The World Is My Canvas

R.I.P. Recovery in Progress

Joe The Poet

(Joe Easterday)

Gotham Books

30 N Gould St.
Ste. 20820, Sheridan, WY 82801
https://gothambooksinc.com/

Phone: 1 (307) 464-7800

© 2025 *Joe Easterday*. All rights reserved.

No part of this book may be reproduced, stored in a retrieval system, or transmitted by any means without the written permission of the author.

Published by Gotham Books (January 3, 2025)

ISBN: 979-8-3482-6900-5 (H)
ISBN: 979-8-3482-6925-8 (P)
ISBN: 979-8-3482-6926-5 (E)

Because of the dynamic nature of the Internet, any web addresses or links contained in this book may have changed since publication and may no longer be valid.

The views expressed in this work are solely those of the author and do not necessarily reflect the views of the publisher, and the publisher hereby disclaims any responsibility for them.

CONTENTS

A Daughters Fairytale 2
A Dream from the Dark 4
A Poem Like This 6
ABC's 12
Agape 15
An Ode to Mother 19
"Basement" 21
Bathroom 26
Better Left Unsaid 28
Brotherhood 31
"A Candy Story" 34
Darkness Surmises 38
Destiny 39
"Discernment" 42
Doin' Time 45
From Me 47
"Dragon" 50
"Driven By Ambition" 52
"FROM ME" 56
God Gave Me You 59
"Goodbye" 62
I Just Did Cid 64
I Didn't Mean To 67
"I Fall for Angels" 72
I Get Lonely with You 74
I Hate the Way That I Love You 77
'I HATE YOU" 79
"I Promise" 82
I Push You Away 84
I Strive 87
"I'm Sorry" 89
Inside Our Dreams 91
Is Me 93
"Isabella" 95
King & Queen 97
"Lighthouse" 99

Love Defined	102
Love	106
"May This Family Thrive"	108
Medicine	110
Meet in The Middle	113
"My Brittle Disease"	116
My Brother's Keeper	119
"My Distorted Reflection"	121
My Eulogy	125
My Mother's Strength	127
My Own Maze	130
My True Love for You	133
Never Forget You	137
"Nothing Left"	140
Oh Faceless One	142
Ouija Board	145
Outkast	148
"Overcome"	152
Pain So Real	154
"People Are Equal"	156
Pills Kills	159
Psychopaths Diary	162
Quiet Noize	165
Razors Edge	168
"Reel Eyes"	171
"Roses Are Dead"	173
Russian Roulette	175
"Sacred Wisdom"	178
Sometimes	181
Stain of Pain	184
"Suicide Ride"	186
Target	188
"Teller"	191
"The 3 Ps of Me"	193
The Addicts Prayer	195
The Backpack Man	197
"The Bastard Pastor"	200
The Box Is Locked	204
The Break Up	206

The Devil's Love Letter	208
The Evil Needle	210
The Games Over	213
"The Lonely Man"	216
The Next Prison Letters	218
The Power of Pain	221
These Bars	224
This Is My Life	226
This Lonely Road	232
"TIRED"	236
To My Mama	238
To My Pops (David Hartman)	240
"Together We Stand"	243
Tongue Twister	245
"Twisted Thoughts"	247
"Unstable"	251
Vacant Says the Sign	253
Veinfull	256
"Voices"	259
What Is Insane?	262
"When I Saw You"	265
"When She Smiles"	269
Will You Stay?	271
You Followed Me	274
You're All That I Need	276

This book is dedicated to my daughter
Isabella Raelynn Easterday

Daddy loves you baby girl, you're the best thing to ever bless my life!

I wanted to take this time to thank all my family and friends and any of my close loved ones. Anyone that has showed me support and encouraged me to do this journey and take these steps of becoming an author. Thank you I love you and although you are my fans I just want you to know that I am your fan to I couldn't have done it without you. Most of all I want to take this time to write someone very special to me and give her the well deserved credit she needs. The beautiful Mother of my daughter, Allison. I know some of you may be wondering why I don't have tons of poems written about her and she wonders that to. Well it's simple as talented and creative as I am I simply cannot come up with anything good enough for such a wonderful woman. She is the greatest person I have ever had in my corner and I cannot thank her enough. She has always been there for me whenever I needed her and without question or regret. Even when I didn't deserve her she was still there. She has put up with way more of my bullshit than any woman should ever have to and for that I can never write anything meaningful enough that could ever express exactly how I felt about this woman, I HAVE TRIED! I just can't find any justifying words or expressive sentences to tell her what she means to me. There's a few of my poems that I wrote for her but I still think they are nothing along the lines of what I wanted to say and for her to hear. So I just want you to know that you are the light that keeps me going the drive that pushes me forward and the motivation I have always needed to want to do better in life. Giving me my daughter is the greatest gift you could have ever given me and for that I can never show you enough gratitude and appreciation. I love you and this book and any success I have in the future and wherever this takes me in my career and in my life is my never ending poem to you baby I hope that means something to you. You will always be my everything and no one can ever take your place, you are my heart, mind, body and soul and reasons why I am alive today.

Thank You Babe

Life has a funny way of revealing itself to us when we least expect it. Through endless twist and turns, down miles of pain and anguish, decades of disappointment and deceit. Misery is a milestone that can be marked throughout the history of every one of our trivial existences. Struggles come and go like a daily event and can almost be scheduled with the type of lifestyles we choose to live. However the imprint that we leave on this world and the ones who we leave behind are truly what matters. Your life is written in a timeline categorized almost like a book. There are chapters to your life and just because the first half of your book was a shit show and a complete disgrace to you or anyone that matters to you doesn't necessarily mean the remaining chapters have to be written without a happy ending. As we grow older we find out lessons on our own, more so than not we learn those lessons the hard way. Yet those lessons tend to show us that our lives are pathways of what we choose to pave. Our journey is only obstructed by what we allow to limit us within ourselves and the people, places, and things that we let into our lives that equally distract us from our goals and dreams. Your future is set forth and bound by the chains that we ourselves let confine us. Everyone is unique and this crazy world we live in is diverse. There are many evils within it that corrupt the purity of humanity and all of society. Our morals that we have lost sight of so long ago that were once kind, caring, and compassionate have become polluted with sin and drugs, disrespect and betrayal. Loyalty seemingly is the easiest trait to have yet the hardest one to find. Greed over rides all of man's desires and is bridled with lust and selfishness. As we see our newer generations sink further into this madness we do nothing to stop the poison that is programed into their minds by the media and within our schools of today. The movements of the masses designed solely to create division and hatred is propaganda that is not only a trending topic to tele market but it fattens the pockets of so many while destroying the lives of millions while they sit back and watch their carefully calculated plans unravel. The world has become a wicked system of a carefully played chess game of professionals against beginners. Knowing the opponents next moves before they even make them and they know the inevitable outcome. I was a pawn in that game for so long yearning to become great yet fumbling with greater players painstakingly losing match after match to my many opponents. Those same competitors turned out to be my many demons. My struggles and lessons in life have come to me at a time when I needed them to hit me the most. A time when life was rearing its worst situations and lowest points of no return right in my face nose to nose point blank. The usual parts where most men decided they couldn't handle this game of life and suicide was the only option. The thought of death seemed a peaceful calm to all this madness that I helplessly was facing. A final cease to all the Hell to which I was utterly trapped under the abyss. My own mental asylum of captivity that was controlling me. A shroud of darkness that blanketed my soul with no relief from my own sorrows and guilt. The failures and mistakes I had made in life were so heavy that they weighed on me daily. A constriction that was a constant reminder that I saw every time I looked in the mirror that I was a junkie and would always hurt myself and everyone around me. Prison was my home and was a lonely desolate island made of all my past endeavors that always ended with setbacks and pain. Resulting in loss and disappointment, my hurt was eternal and I was never going to be good enough or ever find love or happiness. My only sense of joy or pleasure came from the pin prick of that needle and the toxic contents inside. This seemed to be my only natural ability and talent was to tear down every good thing I ever built in my life, and it all came from one terrible monster that I had let take over me. It was my codependency on anything mind altering mainly anything I could put inside of my arms. My drug addiction didn't start because I was out experimenting and trying to fit in by partying and wanting to be the cool kid. In fact I played football for several years and suffered a severe back injury. An injury that ultimately led to the doctors whom I thought I could trust that went to school for longer than I had been alive to be the best at what they do, to heal and give me the best medical care possible. Instead, not only was my football career over but my career of addiction was just beginning. Having been prescribed OxyContin at the age of fourteen. At that time I grew up with the D.A.R.E. (Drug Abuse Resistance Education) program and knew to stay away from drugs but without any education on the dangers of how quickly and easily you can become dependent on prescription pain pills I quickly found out that addiction does not discriminate on your age, sex, race, religion, or creed. It doesn't matter who what when or where you come from you can fall victim to this disease just as easily as I did and in the blink of an eye. It started with pain pills fed to me like candy by overpaid doctors that are sworn to save lives and heal our communities. A few years later the circles of friends grew the crowds and parties got bigger, my thirst for more along with that urge to push the limits fueled with the depression that floods any addict led me to trying new things. Weed, Cocaine, Crack, Acid, Shrooms, PCP, Heroin, Inhalants, every Opiate that you can think of Benzos, and of course drinking. If I could catch a buzz from something I was in. You name it I've done it! Obviously the rest of the terrible things that come with that lifestyle also followed. I have had numerous overdoses, countless close friends that I've had to bury from deadly overdoses including girlfriends that I loved dearly. Tens of thousands of dollars wasted on drugs, priceless items that can never be replaced that I traded off for dope, that can never be replaced with any amount of money because they were sentimental. All the people I have hurt all the permanent damage I've done to the ones I truly love and all the damage I've done to my body over the years. I've legally died and had to be brought back before from a lethal cocktail of Methadone and Xanax. I started going to prison which only fueled my rage and my addiction, along with toxic connections that grew into enormous problems for me as well. I was introduced to a prison Gang and just really went down the wrong path over the next ten years. Every time I thought I had it under control and my life would reach an all-time crazy or a newer rock bottom I would somehow manage to top that by a new low the very next time by getting arrested again and ending right back in that same position I just left from. I ended up robbing pharmacies just to support my habit, and was blasted all over Google as the "Pharmacy Bomb Robber". They labeled me as this monster, when really I was just a struggling addict who ultimately needed help. I don't know if you have ever been arrested let alone been to prison but when you have been to prison four times like I have you really start kicking yourself in the ass after a while and wondering if this is just the hand your dealt. That moment when I would be placed in the back of that cop car and I was hand cuffed I always remembered every second of those car rides because I knew in my mind whatever the next chapter of my life had planned for me it involved years maybe even decades in prison once again. I wouldn't make it out more than six to eight months so I spent my entire 20s locked up every single year. Finally after four prison bits I came home was on six months of house arrest, got a great job welding, got promoted, and bought a really nice car. I ended up completing house arrest, and I was doing so well. My criminal life and past was behind me and I thought I would never have to worry about it ever again, I could move forward and begin a brand new life... or so I thought! Until I met HER!!! I met a girl named Crystal who came into my life and destroyed my entire existence and crumbled every piece of hope that I achieved. Any glimpse of success that my future had any reason to be brighter or any accolades of proud moments that I could look back on all gone burnt up in the ashes of a faded memory tarnished by this one last drug that ruled them all. Crystal Meth. Her shards had a hold of me unlike anything I ever experienced before and once I pushed that poison into my veins that rush hit me and my life was never the same. My thought patterns changed, my ideas grew, my charisma climbed as well as my ego which was at an all-time high. My emotions and feelings seemed to die and fade and my already immense work ethic tripled to an extreme level that made me look like Superman. "Why have I not done this shit before?" I thought. My favorite part was I didn't have the urge to do use any other drug, you couldn't give me a pain pill! I justified my new-found addiction as a positive quality because in my mind it took away all my other addictions to drugs that I knew was going to kill me that had already taken my life once before. I never could have been more wrong!

Methamphetamine was and will always be my biggest and worst demon. I was the absolute worst version of myself on that wicked drug and I can't believe how long it had ahold of me. It caused nothing but turmoil to my life. I've watched so many of my friends waste their entire life and throw everything away for that drug as well. Before I knew It I was living back at my Mom's with nothing! Single, depressed, and strung out once again fighting my biggest battle yet with addiction. I remember sitting in the bathtub one morning and getting a phone call from someone from the hospital it was a recovery coach of that E.R. and she was telling me my chart just happened to come across her morning report and it appeared to her that I was apparently a professional drug addict and it was obvious to her that I needed help. Little did I know that was the best phone call I would ever receive and it would eventually change my life. That conversation soon changed to me getting to know my recovery coach on a personal level and maybe a little against the hospitals HIPPA laws and guidelines we started seeing each other. You can't help who you fall in love with though so screw you HIPPA! We soon moved in together and she changed my whole outlook on life. She gave me purpose and a fire inside I've never felt before I ended up getting a job driving for the Amish and becoming very close friends with one family in particular that to this day are close friends of mine. They bought me my own vehicle and basically made me part of their family. I was driving over 70 plus hours a week and things were looking up at this time it was amazing I was off the drugs and doing what I was supposed to be for once in my life I was happy and I was proud. Then It all started to unravel once again. That itch started to come back, my side girl kept whispering in my ear to come see her, how she missed me and I cannot lie when I say that I also missed her. I missed my Crystal! To make things even worse the woman I was seeing had lost her job at the hospital because people had found out about our relationship and turned her in to management, so she was fired due to dating a client which made me feel super depressed and guilty and drove me further into believing that it was ok to numb my pain away with that substance. Times got tough my girlfriend and I had several arguments and fights I would move out or she would leave for several days and we just couldn't get along. Our relationship was failing and I was slacking in my jobs in driving and so I went back to my old habits and old groups of friends and began selling drugs to not only support my habit but also to try and support the bills. Even with all the money I was making off of driving full time, drug dealing, and hustling anything I could on the side it was never enough and eventually we got evicted but not before we found out we were going to have our first baby together. That really was exciting and nerve racking all at the same time. Here we were our life in shambles I'm in the streets selling and using dope, my family had disowned me at the time, I'm lying and covering up my addiction to all my close Amish friends who really cared about me and had my best interest, and now I have a baby on the way. We were being evicted with nowhere to go, my life in ruins and I don't know what to do. I did the only thing I could and knew how to do and I turned to my dearly beloved mistress Crystal for all the answers and the end result was me getting arrested once more! This time getting my Amish friends vehicle that they bought for me impounded with drugs found not only in the vehicle but on myself as well facing a level four felony and once again, being placed in hand cuffs and in the back seat of that cop car hauled off on my way to jail with the haunting thought that I am going away for years and may miss out on not just the birth of my daughter but the entire first half of her whole life. My world was devastated and it was all my doing once again. Look what I have done! How many people are going to be effected by my decisions yet again and how can I ever explain this. Who is going to be there and why would I ever deserve anyone anyway? I deserve everything coming to me. My baby girl is going to be calling someone else her daddy, why didn't I listen to anyone? These were all the thoughts running through my head as I was being hauled off to jail once more. After being booked in I laid there on that jail floor contemplating suicide and hating myself more than I ever have before, despising my addiction and all that it has taken from me. Wishing that I had never met Crystal and that ruin the bitch had left me in ever since she took my life and drug me straight to Hell with her. I wanted to die and never have I ever felt so alone. Even when I cried out to God with tears pouring down my face I still felt and heard nothing. I can't begin to tell you what a hollow shell of a man you become and how empty and alone you truly are when you beg God just to hear you and you have lived in sin for so long that even he won't listen. Again this was all my doing though it was all my fault and I had no one to point any fingers at but myself I couldn't be angry with anyone but my own damn self and for the first time in my life I could solemnly admit that I was wrong. The way I was living, the things I was doing, the attitude I had, my habits, my ideas, my patterns, my beliefs, my mentality, my devotions, my commitments and loyalties everything about who I was all wrong and for the first time I knew that I didn't like the person I had become and in order for me to have any chance at life or freedom from drugs or a shot at happiness I had to be willing to let go of all that selfishness and pride. All my unrighteous behaviors and the trailing's with women that I couldn't resist, all my vengefulness, all my anger towards others, all my street mentality and criminal thinking, my friends that I thought were cool and fun and that I just clicked with, all the people who only seemed to be around when I had drugs and most importantly I had to surrender completely to God. So as I lay there on that cold jail floor with all these thoughts running through my mind cut off from the outside world unknowing what my outcome would be I was given my second chance I was bonded out and my brother and the mother of my child were right there telling me that they would be there along this journey as long as I was willing to help myself so I went the next morning and checked myself into a place called Avenues Recovery for intensive inpatient treatment and it was hands down the greatest program to ever be established. That place not only helped me recover but it taught me about myself, my problems, who I am, and who I need to be without drugs. It taught me how to forgive myself and that I wasn't alone. I ended up leading the NA/AA groups within the facility and people really enjoyed how I ran the groups and hearing my lessons. To hear someone that's an addict both younger than myself and twice my age come up to me and say that I really changed their lives and my message impacted them so deeply started a part of recovery for me that I will forever continue. My journey has just begun and I am so thankful for this opportunity as I write this I am two months clean, but by the time you read this (whoever you are) I pray to see years of sobriety. If you or anyone you know is struggling with drugs or alcohol you are not alone in this, please speak up. There are so many people just like you that are or have went through the exact same thing, if not worse. Your same trials and tribulations, the heartache and pain fear and disappointment, the shame and guilt. Days can be tough and the nights can be even harder but let someone help you because drugs and alcohol do not have to rule you anymore. You are strong, you are smart, beautiful, and can accomplish every last one of your hopes and dreams it's just how far your willing to go for that level of success. There is a soldier inside us all we just have to find the worth and motivation to get back up. It's never easy but it's not impossible. I believe in you and your success is my motivation. You owe it to yourself! I love you and I'm here for you so don't give up please reach out to me if there's anything I can help you with I will be praying for you all and thank you so much for all your love and support. I do this for YOU, my family, and anyone out there who can relate to my story and poetry....

Thank You and God Bless!

This was a story I did for a close friend of mine who I was in prison with. His daughter was his world and he wanted to write her a letter and needed a poem with it that made her feel special and remind her she was daddies little Princess. This sparked the idea about the fairytale and the Princess in the story. Later to end up having a Princess of my very own that I could dedicate this to as well. I love you Baby Girl.

A Daughters Fairytale

Once upon a time in a place far away
Your daddy was placed in a cage to stay
Where witches in gloom would zoom on their broom
While cackling with laughter whilst under the moon
Evil consumes this entire place
Darkness surrounds it's strange and deranged
Not a single moment not a day went by
That I didn't miss my princess being by my side
The pain is too much and my eyes flood with tears
As days turn to months and the months to years
In a mystical world of fairytale dreams
Lived a beautiful girl my lovely little Queen
Riding the rainbows colorful light
Unicorns fly high through the bright blue sky
I had wished for a gift which came true
I asked for an Angel and I was given you
So may your dreams be magical you're never alone
I love you princess and I'll soon be home

Don't really have an explanation for this just started with a few words and it transpired to a hidden description of secrets of our government and the elite and the controversial synapsis that they intentionally control under our noses. Don't ask me how it came to be, it just came out of nowhere. Everyone that reads this or hears it will have their own meaning and opinion about this one. It's just me being creative and expressive with my vocabulary. Truth can be found by the investigator and his willingness to be open-minded. Being deceived and manipulated by phantoms that are masked and cloaked is almost a certainty. However the deceiver is he who wears that mask as their own burden that burden will eventually come to pass as a unveiled curse of earthy incite that will enlighten us all one day but knowledge and wisdom comes from the a universal intuition within.

A Dream from the Dark

Secrete the kindness, for reasons decided Perceived as weak as spineless

We weep in a heap of frightened migrants

Scream from our dreams as we bleed in a timeless crisis, please we need our seed to repeat don't deplete politeness, we must keep what guides us, societies stained the sheets that we each used to sheath and hide us, yet it Bleached our eyelids, they speak through their teeth with obscene surprises... so, to those that are woke they may reach but can't find us!!!

"A Poem Like This" was one I did for a talent show that I did that wasn't just set off one topic or idea I guess. I really just wanted to too show off my linguistics and rhyming capabilities. I was in prison at the time and everyone already nicknamed me the Eminem of DOC so I had to live up to that title. The start of the poem I wanted to create this façade that my poem was poorly composed and was corny as shit then to change it on the next verse. Since everyone knew I always had something really intricate, it was a confusing but entertaining transition.

A Poem Like This

(written in voice of illiterate child-like vocabulary and grammar)

WhEn eye w@s a KiD anD thEn i got biG
I nEvEr thoght eYe WUld b ınside of @ fenCe
TalkiNg on tHe foNe 2 mY p@rentz
ınStead of bEıng Home 2 helP w!th reNt
bUt im @ Litle imbarased ladyes & jents
CaUsE EyE kNow u wa$nt xpEktIng "A poem liKe tHi$"

(Normal Intellectual vocabulary and speech)

Aww forget it, my mind can't write this simplicit
It's distant and twisted so nonfiction it glistens
My monologue is animalistic intricate with his linguistics
You can't get a grip or miss this depiction
I go and get it, solo no codependent, so just listen
If you don't know then just show attention
Cause the flows exquisite, mind blown ballistic
A broke commission this gross hope shows no description
So unique and distinct that even my clone is different

My thoughts never rest and its quite the test
Despite his type we don't like to address
Cause his rhymes and dialect have this violent effect
To insight a riot with slight suspect to which might upset
They say the way I write is alright I guess
His wordplay is great but it's not the best

So try as you might but I'm not impressed

Cause I'm your basic entertainment, invasive in my derangement
Enraged but it's lament, vacant and so complacent
Serrated as a blade that's been made to be abrasive
Tame but its belated, he's strange and its fragrant
Anxious in amazement, I'm gracious with my patience
Insane and I can't fake it there's graves in my basement
Encased with this pain, as I embrace the containment
Plagued with defrayment, I may be straight from Satan
Chasin the array of arraignment, I'd face it but I'm faceless
An alien whose brain is so frayed it's been paved with contagion

All these vivid illusions, with different conclusions
Wicked intrusions, of sickened contusions
Twisted with bruises, that's missin' its distant sentiment of an imminent protrusion
Intimate fluid you can see through this dudes translucence as I piss pollution
I'm laughin' as your blastin' this blasphemous music
I make broken improvements to focus delusions
Grotesque solutions makes for the best resoultions
Hopefully my poetry ain't going to be a nuisance
I know my vocabulary is scary and putrid, it's very gruesome
Just real quick that means sick in case you're stupid
But even with all these loose screws don't jump to conclusions
Cause I can change it up and still be fluent

So listen close to my approach of the atonement
Of my sins I cannot win and once again I am hopeless

Duly noted, my opponent, I may grin but I can't focus
You make question this suggestion indigestion overdosin'
I'm not boastin, I'm exposin, these words spoken keeps you goin
Nose to nose Joe's show boatin', always gloatin'
Head is swollen it's always growin' that's the notion
My emotion floods the ocean fully loaded I'm not jokin'
Pistons glowin', business smokin', omnipotent cryptic decoded
And just as quick I flip the script on the direction that I've chosen

I had to walk through hell on a broken leg, and I often fell along my quest
Where I plead for help as I'd scream and beg,
and alone I'd yell in the land of dead
But the misery swells when there's no one else to press
It's an empty well that's black and depressed, and in fact at best
It's hard to understand when there's no one left, I'm a broken man I never planned to confess
I held my grandma as she took her last breath and it felt like a bullet had bruised my chest
So I aim at my veins as I shoot with meth, playin' Russian roulette I don't care about death
I use to seek solace as I'd look to cope
Like that day that my brother didn't answer his phone
So I went to go see him, he was home all alone
No one knew he was depressed and he had lost all hope
So there he hung as he swung dead from the rope
His neck was stretched and he began to bloat
Had to cut him down and I just couldn't cope
We locked eyes one last time and that's all she wrote
I remember screamin' at God as I'd nod off on dope

Then I got stuck with that lethal needle, drugs are bad but that syringe is evil

It makes me cringe till I'm weak and feeble, it ruined my life and it killed my people

Yet I'm still looking at life through the eye of a peephole

If you can't understand that metaphor then come tweak with me

You'll lose weight and forget to eat, you'll be scared to blink and afraid to leave

And we'll each lose sleep for at least three weeks

But I'm not glorifying this life this is my disease

I remember being so low that I'd drop to my knees

As I'd try and plead, I'd cry and scream

I'd try to fry my mind where I'd lie and bleed

On the floor of course no remorse for a fiend

It's like I'm forced to feed, to support my need

All while beggin' and prayin' for a few reliefs, just a new release, a different view at least

Cause I feel like a useless piece, I've lost dozens of loved ones from deadly OD's

Not to mention for instance my recent B, took 45 of my life cause I tried Ms. D

So the lessons learned is that it hurts to grieve

Now let's avert your attention so it's not on me

We'll change the speech although equally deep

My hearts relentless on the parts that I've chosen to vent

And the acquisitions to my addiction was a spoken event

It's almost over and I know that you was hopin' I'd quit

But I won't diminish the existence of my persistence till I've finished my skit

So let me refocus my approach as we conclude to an end
And yes I'm grinning because I've just proven that omens exist
I wasn't kidding at the beginning when I said you wasn't expecting "A Poem Like This"

This next one is a very corny but cute love poem called ABC's I wanted to take the alphabet and see if I could write it into a love poem so this is my creation.

ABC's

A - is for absolute just like my love for you

B - represents beauty you're so sexy to me boo

C - to me means couple, and we go so good it's got to be true

D - is for die cause if it wasn't for you that just what I'd do

E - is for elevate, picking me up when I'm sad and when I'm blue

F - for forever together like these letters side by side <u>***U and I***</u> should be too

G - means great like a team we relate you're my dream and its fate

H - cause you're from Heaven God can't make mistakes

I - is irresistible and I always want a taste

J - for the joy that you consistently create

K - since your kind I thank the lord you're all mine

L - symbolizes love and ours is one of a kind

M - to show matrimony that was so easy to decide

N - narrates the story of our lives and I get told a fairytale every time we lock eyes

O - cause you're the only one under the sun I've never run from

P - for patience before you I had none

Q - since you're my Queen this King does come

R - cause you're righteous and you roll off my tongue

That says she pleaded & cried
As she tried to recite from the good book
Right before she died
It's been some time since her life got took

         I suffer derangement
        Locked away in containment
          You stay in my chains
        While I play with your brains
         Alone in my "<u>Basement</u>"

A door opens & you're blinded by the bright light
That shines bright down the stairs
You scream & it seems the beams only gleams
As a shadow stands there
It's got to be me who else could it be
But all you see
Is the silhouette & facial hair
You're visions impaired
You're trembling scared
Scream if you dare no one will care
I can almost taste it, my new patient
Inside of my "<u>Basement</u>" in the middle of nowhere

         I suffer derangement
        Locked away in containment
         You stay in my chains
        While I play with your brains
         Alone in my "<u>Basement</u>"

S - since our sex is the best I can't get enough

T - cause to me you're true through and through I'm obsessed

U - understand you're so different from the rest

V - has me vexed like how you're still cute when you're upset

W - means we and together forever we shall be

X - is what those other bitches are, why you think I wrote these ABCs

Y - has to be you because without you I can't breathe

Z - means zero for real though without you there is no me

Now I said my ABCs next life won't you be with me?

This poem was written for my Daughter the first few nights after I found out that I was going to have a kid. I didn't even know if we were going to have a boy or girl yet so I ended up having to change it later when I wrote it like I was having a boy but then found out it was a little girl. She became my princess and I love her all the same Agape if you don't know what that means it's the love the God has for us and the level and amount of his love.

Agape

For So long I've been lost looking for a beacon
A direction in life, a 2nd chance or a reason
Something so powerful it could conquer my demons
A sudden rush or gust of love that's unconditionally needed

Day after day I would pray you would be sent to me
As life passed by through my eyes
The seasons seemed to be leaving me almost instantly
So the sadness and drugs increased with the urge to OD
Along with being driven by destruction and an abundance of the penitentiary
And I would only receive another gift-less misery
Year after year my need for you became imminent to see
I'd hit a shot watch the clock and the empty spot underneath the Christmas tree

I was an arbitrary assignment of solitary confinement
A tornado of torment an adornment of defiant

Chaos and madness just happened to be the norm
Yearning for your love or just a touch of your pure form
Begging for a reason to keep breathing instead of swinging from a cord
Hurting daily just waiting for a baby of my own to be born

And what's more, I've been with women who pretended, said I was the father for sure

I can't ever explain the pain when you find out it isn't yours
The soul isn't designed to survive that level of torn
So I had nothing to live for not even the Lord

But I promised God a long time ago
Give me this gift, please because I'm so alone
For if you do I will change my life
I can't go on much more I could die tonight

I gave up hope as I grouped onto the dope It was the only relief that allowed me to cope

And as time added up behind those bars
I lost all faith I faded away with my heart

But miracles can happen they say if you believe
And when those two lines appeared on that test I was in complete disbelief
The answer to my prayers my gift under the tree
A soothing relic that angelic need
An offering of an offspring grown from my seed
A child of my own on her way to me

I couldn't prepare myself for this precious blessing
I instantly let go of all that's depressing

I've been through unbearable agony and countless close calls
But it was all for a purpose and that was to give you my all

I haven't done anything to ever deserve you

So I will obliterate anyone that tries to hurt you

I'll hold you and protect you with the bare flames on my back
I'd stand in front of a train just to heal your pain, lay down and die on those tracks

My unyielding love for you is an emotion that new
But its opened my eyes to a brand new view

I'd suffer the storm and go to war with any force
I'd walk through the rain all day just so you'd never want anymore
I'd fall with the fall just to dissolve all your pain of course

No matter how many times I try to recite it
Practice, reread it, erase it, or retype it
Look for a vice, think twice, and decide to rewrite it
It's useless because I just can't do it without cry

You're the only thing that matters along with God above
You soften the heart of this violent thug
Filling that void that I used to destroy with drugs
The most addicting thing will be your innocent hugs
You have my heart and my soul and I can't express enough
"Agape" can't even describe this type of love

This was something I just wrote for my Mom wishing her a Happy birthday and it was something I wrote for a lot of people to send on cards to their Moms for their Birthdays when I was in prison but Just know Mother I wrote this specifically for your old bitter ass I love you (ps to all the readers if you ever suffer an ailment of any sort just drink lemon water.... Cure ya right up) -Inside joke with me and my Mom.....

An Ode to Mother

Love comes in levels but there's one like no other
And it comes from a Son when he loves his Mother

I would suffer all your sorrows and take all the blame
I would die for my Mother just to take away her pain

Words can't describe or express the degree
Of the type of relationship between my Mother and me

A woman of strength often hides her misery
But that's part of a Mother's overall victory

Cause some people suffer from the weight of their chains
But a Mother can break through to us no matter the restraints

Through all the sports I had my Mother's support
My whole life I was raised by a hero of sorts

To express my gratitude would be easy to say
But to show you Mother there's just no way

My Mother's forgiving even when impossible to conquer
The Angels in Heaven can't even compare or top her

But the man that I am can be sold as new
Happy Birthday Mother this is an ode to you

Another crazy one that is a bit deranged and written from the minds of a serial killer. I thought it would be interesting to write a poem from the stand point of a serial killer like Jeffery Dahmer, John Wayne Gacy, Ted Bundy, Richard Ramirez, or Ed Gein. What would a poem sound like written from one of them? What depiction would the reader get if they read files from one of these psychopaths own journals? This is my poem I wrote in that sense.

"Basement"

> I suffer derangement
> Locked away in containment
> You stay in my chains
> While I play with your brains
> Alone in my "<u>Basement</u>"

The rats won't let you sleep
As they sneak & creep & constantly squeak
How long have you been down here?
At least a week you think!
All you have to drink is the stagnant water
That's discolored & reeks
Then there's a pale of raw rotten meat
That the freak gave you to eat & it stinks
You can't stop the chatter of your teeth
As you listen to the clatter of feet
While the floor boards creak
Above your head so you try not to speak....

> I suffer derangement
> Locked away in containment
> You stay in my chains
> While I play with your brains
> Alone in my "<u>Basement</u>"

You yank on the chains
As you gaze around this room

It's full of gloom
You're amazed you can still move
You refuse to accept doom
But what the fuck can you do?
And who is this dude who captured you?
Each time this freak seems to come through
He don't speak he just sings a new tune
As he stares at you, cause you're bloody & bruised
Covered in your own shit & piss too
The surrounding walls are covered in sharp tools
Dripping from crud, rust, & blood
These instruments are all to crude
I haunt you & taunt you by the thought
Of which one I might use....

         I suffer derangement
        Locked away in containment
          You stay in my chains
        While I play with your brains
         Alone in my "<u>Basement</u>"

Curled in a ball, you're scared & shook
You notice the body parts in the dark
That hang from hooks
The smell lingers as the fingers
Sway with a crook
You squint to see a dead granny
Missin panties that's crammed in a nook
Her swollen bloated face
Has this terrible look

One by one down the stairs I come
Terrified embraced by chains for days
You try & hide but there's nowhere to run
As you scream at me to leave
And what the fuck do I want
I just smile & hum
As I ruthlessly chew on a piece of used gum
There I stand a strange & deranged man
Pistol in hand I cock the hammer with my thumb
I bellow with laughter my weapon flashes as brain matter splashes
Boom goes the gun....

So just breathe there's no need
To complain about your placement
You're stuck, you're fucked
You might as well face it
Sick twisted & demented
Is the figment of this statement
And tonight you die
Inside the confines of my
"<u>Basement</u>"

For whatever reason the bathroom always feels like the safest place to be while you are a tweaker and addicted to meth I don't know why this is or what causes our minds to think this way but I would find myself stuck in the bathroom for days and so I had to write a poem dedicated to this. Looking back now that I am sober I am so thankful that I only need a bathroom for the normal uses like regular people.

Bathroom

Inside this room I am free
A place to play that's hard to leave
Where I can shoot up, shit, shower, and pee
Look in the mirror what do I see
Huge pupils black as can be

Paranoid and window peakin'
Eyes so dry my teeth are clickin'
Mouth so wide, I can hear them blinkin'
Down, upside, and backwards thinkin'
See what I mean, why do I keep tweakin'

So here I go to this "Bathroom" alone
A serene security and comforting home
My peace of mind in my peaceful zone
Active status online shown
Stuck on the toilet, stuck on the phone

Rinsing the rig, blood in the sink
Finely feet as I chatter my teeth
Shaky knees as I try to breathe
My soothing sanctuary, it's my safe keep
In this "Bathroom" is where I tweak and geek

This was a story I created to address awareness on both issues for woman and children that they both have to go through. The horrors that kids and women suffer every day and the trauma they have to live with after that type of mental, physical, and sexual abuse. It's a sad story but I want people to know this type of reality exist and this is the life for some people.

Better Left Unsaid

Don't take this light or mild cause everything in life isn't always bright with smiles. The ways of the world are wicked and vile and this is about a sick pedophile that defiled a child...

Daddy went berserk, committed suicide is what she heard.
Her mother was a junkie that used to trick and twerk for work
And would hit her when the percs ran out of her purse but
To make things worse, would always leave her alone with men that were perverse. So she'd run down the street and hide at the church as she'd sit and swing from the tire that hung high on the birch. Everyone knew that this child had worth but like a rose that grows and gets trampled in the dirt, what has she done to deserve such a curse? It's not her fault she didn't ask for her birth. She always feels pain and blame and constant hurt it's so absurd.

She's too young to be contemplating suicide, she has such a fragile mind, looking up towards the sky, she begins to cry and wonders why she feels so dead inside she pictures a new life as she wishes she just died.

She fades away into a fable day dream and pictures what being a little girl really means. Pigtails, fairytales, makeup dress up and earrings. Playing with barbies, tea parties, and princess things. Then she snaps back from all the make believe to her own Hell on earth that seems so obscene.

Then one day her dope fiend Mom came to say, "stay here and play and I'll be back in a few days, I got a friend that will watch you while I'm away. The two of you will get along just great I promise it's ok, be good and don't stay up too late". Not that she really cared about her daughters fate, her only concerns were the drugs she was about to take.

Alone in her room it's close to three, she's watching TV. Her Mom's friend enters eagerly asking if she's hungry as he offers her something to eat. She was starved to death so she accepts his treat. It tasted kind of funny it seemed way too sweet. Next thing she knows she awakes from a deep sleep and screams. There's blood on the covers her knees, and sheets, it registers immediately but she's to scared to speak, she thinks to herself "how could this happen to me I just turned thirteen?" She was raped in her bed and she feels so unclean, it hurts to move and stings when she pees who was that creep and what does this mean? Who could she tell about that freak and who would listen or ever believe? No one would care so she decides to leave as she ran away to live life on the streets. She barely had clothes or shoes on her feet, she's alone and cold no money to eat and under a bridge is where she'd freeze trying to sleep. And there in the night she would cry and weep as she'd pray every night for her sorrow to cease. Then she got sick, it became hard to breathe, medical attention is what she needs, so she checks into a hospital and is quickly seen by medical teams. Turns out she's pregnant almost eighteen weeks, but there's something else as they run an IV. The results she receives has her hitting her knees as she screams and pleads. "JESUS PLEASE I JUST GOT DONE BEIN A PRE-TEEN WHY ME?" The man who raped her has disease and now her and her baby both have HIV and the babies born deceased because her bodies too weak to let her conceive.

So let me ask you was this true or made up instead? Was the girl real and really raped in her bed? Did she and the baby get aids and is the innocent baby really dead? Can kids live lives so mislead? Let these questions linger for a moment inside of your head. Because some things in life are not just some shit you read, and some things in life are "Better Left Unsaid".

"Brotherhood" is a meaningful explanation about my views and beliefs on the subject. I take the meaning and representation seriously and use it as a core foundation of my entire being. I stand for it and I base my whole existence off it to illuminate the true meaning of "Brotherhood".

Brotherhood

A true bond forgotten and left behind
A trusting relationship to often denied
A man of his word these days you can hardly find

I'd live for you don't worry
As I'd die for you in a hurry
My Brother's keeper through any storm or any flurry

A Brother is like no other
Even with different past & different mothers
Through thick or thin we both bleed the same color

Dear Brother of mine
When it's time to ride
You don't even have to question if I'll be by your side

Shoulder to shoulder back to back
Us against the world and that's a fact
Well never face our enemies alone we've grown intact

So if you die before I wake, just wait I'm coming too
Well rule the underworld together Brother because Hell was built for two
Even the devil knows better than to separate me and you

My word and my loyalty has meaning with so much depth
Love and trust with the upmost respect

Are all things I give you, none with neglect

So don't be misunderstood
Because if we could we would
Do it for the good of our "Brotherhood"

So this next one is not really a poem but a short story I created that I thought was to funny not to include in my book. Have you ever read those short stories were people write an illustration using references or themes from something totally opposite the spectrum. Using words and manipulating them into something other than what they are intended for? I read a story like this once using candy bars as the topic If you still have no clue as to what I am talking about you will once you read this story... VIEWER DESCRETION ADVISED!

"A Candy Story"

On **Payday Mr. Goodbar** stepped out onto **5th Avenue** showing off his bag full of **100 Grand**. He decided he wanted to hire a hooker so he found a nice **Dark Chocolate** prostitute named **Snickers** but "She" turned out to be a "He". After kicking **Snickers** in his hidden **Chocolate Covered Peanuts, Mr. Goodbar** was on his was to try his luck again. He ran into some gang members that called themselves the **Three Musketeers**. The leader of the gang was called **Rollo**. **Rollo** happened to also be a pimp who told **Mr. Goodbar** that he had a real **Sweat Tart** for him to enjoy **Now & Later**. She was a delicious looking **White Chocolate** bunny that he referred to as **Cookies & Cream. Mr. Goodbar** couldn't resist her the sight of her soft **Marshmallow** skin. **Cookies & Cream** was a real **Gob Stopper. Mr. Goodbar** had to taste that **Pink Starburst** so they headed off someplace private. **Mr. Goodbar** chatted with **Cookies & Cream** along the way as he learned that she also stripped at **Club Soda** and worked as a bar tender down at **Twizzlers**. As she puffed on her **Candy Cigarette Cookies & Cream** started feeling like she could trust **Mr. Goodbar**. Maybe it was the heat getting to her because she was really starting to melt for this **Big Hunk** of a man. She started opening up to him more and more the further they walked. She revealed that **Cookies & Cream** was only her stage and call name, that her real name was **Reese. Mr. Goodbar** couldn't keep his eyes off **Reese's** luscious **Strawberry Shortcake Cherry** lips he could tell she knew her way around a **Jolly Rancher**. They rounded the corner of **Hershey Street**. He lived two blocks from Drury Lane, home of the biggest treat dealer in the city. The notorious **Muffin Man**. Finally arriving at **Mr. Goodbar's Ginger Bread House** after they walked through the rough neighborhood. As soon as they closed the door they started sharing **Kisses** as **Reese** grabbed **Mr. Goodbar's Nuts** making his **Gummy Worm** grow stiff and ridged like a **Chico Stick** and as hard as a **Jaw Breaker**. As **Reese's** mouth began to water for that spicy **Fire Ball. Mr. Goodbar** led **Reese** to his bedroom where they started getting naked, unwrapping each other slowly and delicately. **Mr. Goodbar** couldn't believe what a **Hot Tamale** he had standing before him. He laid her down on his **Cotton Candy** sheets. Her breast were plump and soft as he mashed them together like a couple **Gummy Bears** admiring her **Peach Ring** piercings. They stood erect like little **Candy Corn** as well as **Mr. Goodbar's Hard Candy Butterfinger,** which glistened at its tip like White **Snow Caps.** He felt as firm as a **Heath Bar** and **Reese's Cupcake** was already oozing it's gooey **Cream Filling. Reese** looked up at him with lust in her eyes saying "I want to be your naughty **Nougat Mr. Goodbar!**" Rubbing her **Sweet Syrup** all over the tip of his **Crunchy Butterfiinger** he buried his **Salty Pretzel Rod** deep in her **Honey Bun. Reese** wasn't expecting to be taken in her rear **Butterscotch Button** so she screamed out loud **"OH HENRY!" Mr. Goodbar** was relentless on **Reese's Cow Tail** showing her **Zero** mercy. In the mist of the ravishing she was taking she lost control making a **Mud Pie** all over the **Cotton Candy** sheets. **Reese** coated **Mr. Goodbar's Salted Carmel Nuts** in **Chocolate Pudding**. However he didn't let up even with the sticky mess they were making. Pulling his coated **Pudding Pop** out of **Reese's** back side he carelessly slammed his **Drumstick** into her **Red Velvet** pounding his **Malt Balls** into her Mound. **Her Bit-O-Honey** was too much and he didn't last long spewing his **Milkyway** inside of **Reese.** Seeing his syrup ooze out and mix with this existing mess on the **Cotton Candy** sheets it looked like a pool of **Chocolate Milk.** Growing soft as **Laffy Taffy Reese** gave his **Butterfinger** one last lick tasting his rainbow and savoring it like a **Skittle** showing her appreciation for **Mr. Goodbar** breaking her off like a **Kit Kat.** After getting dressed **Mr. Goodbar** paid **Reese** in **Chocolate Gold Coins** before she left, he also thanked her for their **Nutrageous** time together. He informed her that she was a real **Almond Joy. Reese** told **Mr. Goodbar** to stop by **Club Soda** sometime and she would take him to the VIP section so they could have a **Fast Break.** He said next time he would screw **Reese's Cups** to **Pieces....**

8 months later **Mr. Goodbar** was walking with his new Trick-or-Treat **Peppermint Patty**, who was well known for her **Tootsie Roll**. They had just left the music store after purchasing the new **M&M** cd. They walked together through town waving at a few of their **Peeps**. She couldn't keep her hands off of his **Banana** and was telling him with a smirk on her face, how she had a craving for **Mr. Goodbar's Ice Cream**. Rounding the corner they ran into a very pregnant and very strung out **Reese**. She was walking with her current man she had just scored some **Pop Rocks**. After a brief confrontation **Peppermint Patty** along with **Reese's** new **Sugar Daddy** became annoyed with the situation and decided to leave together. Leaving **Reese** and **Mr. Goodbar** standing there to catch up. After a quick hello **Reese** began begging **Mr. Goodbar** for some cash for their **Baby Ruth**. The junkie still had **Powdered Sugar** on the tip of her nose and she was missing her front **Chicklets**. Reese said if he wanted she would just sell **Mr. Goodbar** their **Sour Patch Kid** for a couple grams of **Milk Duds** or some **Rock Candy**. She said that she had already seen **Dr. Pepper** and he had told **Reese** that their little **Runt** was going to be a girl. **Mr. Goodbar** felt like such an **Air Head** standing there with his prostitute strung out baby mama. **Reese** looking as if she would sell her **Peanut Butter** for just a sip of **Coke**. Ready to **Blow Pop** any **Dum Dum** willing to take a **Fun Dip** in this icky **Wonder Ball**. **Reese** was used up like a piece of chewed up **Bubbalicious**, she started out sweet like **Juicy Fruit** but then lost her flavor and turned disgusting. **Mr. Goodbar** committed suicide later that night because he had such a broken **Candy Heart**. He slit his wrist with a sharpened **Candy Cane** leaving a letter written in his own **Fudge** saying…. "My Sweet Tooth Got The Best Of Me…."

"Darkness Surmises" was just a poem I wrote dedicated to all the evils in the world all the black and wicked things that we see each day and throughout our lives. I just started with this idea of capturing a depiction of what it would look through the eyes of a Godless and cold-hearted emotionless man so this is what I wrote.

Darkness Surmises

Giant surprises
In the eyes of the enlightened
Frightened unrighteous
This need for silence
We keep beside us
It breeds the violence
Deep inside us
The Devils vices
And his evil alliances
That grip and rip and reach behind us
As he precedes to always remind us
The Devil and I resides
In our minds it coincides us
As we comprise the heartless and lifeless
On all the horizons
Shining bright like diamonds
Black and ignited as demons collided
No more shore, no more sunrises
And every breath we breathe "Darkness Surmises"

Destiny

They say fate is fake and make believe
When people meet it was never meant to be
Love is lust and there's so much deceit
That you're weak for wearing your heart on your sleeve
And there's no such thing as *Destiny*...

Your hugs and kisses, your touch and innocence your genuine intentions
I'd go back in an instant just to fix this distance 'cause there's so much I'm missin'...

When I close my eyes to sleep it's you who I see in my dreams
And when I awake I reach for you in these lonely sheets
You make me weak in the knees and my heart skips beats
You bring me peace when it's hard to breath
You're a need so to speak...

I meant what I said the day we wed
You stole my heart and cleared my head
I belong to you 'til the day I'm dead...

It's a love commitment, when you hurt I hurt it's no different...
Through the good times and bad 'til there's nothin' left
I'll cherish my wife 'til the day of my death...
And in the next life I'll wait an eternity for you
Cause Heaven or Hell can't separate us two...
I'll always give you the utmost respect and protection

Never betray or stray or neglect with deception...
We've been through everything under the sun
And I'm so proud of you for all you've done and overcome...
They say beauty is in the eye of the beholder
And you only get more gorgeous as we grow older...
You're my strength and relief to my pain
The air in my lungs and blood in my veins...
I'm blessed as can be that you belong to me
And I don't care what they say...I believe in *Destiny*

I initially wrote this poem as a thank you and appreciation poem to a facilitator of a program I was in while in prison who was really fed up by the way not only the prison staff was running things and conflicting with her teachings and programing but also the way we as her guys were being and a lot of us truly did appreciate her so I wrote this for her. Later I flipped it and edited a few things and changed it into a love poem because I recorded it on my Tiktok and realized it didn't make much sense to anyone who wasn't there so I wanted to direct it more towards my demographic of followers.

"Discernment"

Despite the dealt cards you still played your part
Cause a dog will always fight if you challenge his bark
Cause hatred will rain if you let it burn in your heart
It lights up the night as it shines in the dark

The bottom line is that beauty defined is a duty assigned
It's an amusing disguise usually part of the design
Just like the stars that align in the night sky
Things often happen and we don't know why
No matter how hard you try and you truly fight
Over time the strength resides inside
slowly subsides as it drifts and dies

when our second chances become happened stances that were never meant to happen
cause those same mistakes we made can't be recanted
things change because they never would've lasted
or perhaps the mishaps we just took for granted

lately I've been restless tossin' and turnin', stressin' and uncertain'
if I'm part of the problem, and if I'm really that worthless
you gave me hope, a meaning and a purpose
a new beginning with lessons learned as we earn it
but when you walked out it caused some "discernment"
you leavin' will leave a stain that's permanent

challenges are tough they are rough but worth it
problems can be solved they're all worth workin'
the love that we have was bad at times but nothing is perfect
so give us another chance you know I deserve it

You know how many times I've been asked over the years what prison was like or jail? How did I do all that time what was it like inside of those places and not only does it get annoying having to repeat yourself but also having to relive the same horror stories over and over again when you want nothing more than to just put those timelines from your past behind you... So this is one I wrote to give the best vivid description of what prison was like, and everyone that has ever heard it that has done time in prison has said the same thing. "Yep you nailed it that's word for word the best description for that place when your locked up so if you are wondering what prison is like check this one out!

Also if your reading this and your locked up right now this is dedicated to you and your not forgotten. I've been right there laying in that bunk reading some shit like this right now. That feeling of being stuck and helpless, the unknowing of what's going on the streets. I had no idea I had a path like this but I started planning, setting goals, working hard, and taking action. Focus, ambition and motivation is all you need to change your whole life. I came home from my Fourth prison bit after doing over 10 years total right where you are currently caged at I was there I'm no better than you. I just want to encourage you anything is possible change your life It's worth it. For the lifers that can't come home my thoughts and prayers are with you and your family. That would be hard to accept but you know your heart and where your mind is at today and one day it will end you can still change your life from the inside. Anyone locked up just know the greatest people, the smartest minds, the most creative and artistic, the biggest hearts and mentally toughest people on earth come from Prisons, Jails, and Institutions. Don't give up and I hope my shit puts fire back into you keep pushing you're a soldier men and woman keep surviving and thriving.

Doin' Time

People might drive by and wonder what it's like on the inside
    But it's hard to explain this life when you're "Doin' Time"
This place creates dishonest monsters and pain
    And rehabilitate is just another word for insane
You hear these noises and memorize the sound
    Misery loves company yet that's all you're around
Someone's always watchin' you're under constant stress
    It's a different world when compared to the rest
You can read the people that had nothing on the streets
Cause they hoard everything they see from the salt packets to the linen sheets
The dress code varies from jumpsuits to doo rags
State boots or tennis shoes and whatever you can cram in a bag
Under constant observation, people scheming to take your stuff
    In general population sometimes it gets rough
Everyone's out for themselves they're foul and pretentious
    Chivalry and sympathy are camouflage for their real intentions
Everyday your away is a constant test
    You'll stay with one eye open the sleeps not the best
You have to be trained to go at the drop of a dime
    Keep your shoes tied tight when you're "Doin' Time"
Inmates are cool to your face but they deceive and sneak
    Snakes are fake and they prey on the weak
Your mental stability visually becomes adherent
    Cause these walls and fences will kill your spirit
Paranoia can save your life if you consider the risk

  Because hesitation can get you killed in a place like this
"I got your back" is so easy to say
  But trust is a catastrophe if you give it away
It's supposed to be us against them, the guards I mean
  Yet there's so many J-3s that they play for the wrong team
Convict to convict together as one
  But half of them think they deserve a badge and a gun
Yet the mission of prison is to make me better
  Can you feel me healing from the words of this letter
I just want people to see things from my perspective
  Prison is a place that's dark and deceptive
I'm not seeking sympathy the bad choices were mine
  I'm just trying to describe what it's like "Doin' Time"
Politics and prison go both hand in hand
But it's impossible to be out of the way when you stay in gangland
Nowhere you go can you find privacy
  And you never know who all's a rivalry
It's hard to imagine the madness behind these walls
  There's so much sadness that happens its hard on us all
When you call home and get no answer
  It puts ideas in your head that fester like cancer
It will emotionally break even the strongest of men
  As you count down the calendars until your sentence ends
This place aint for everyone so I hope you listen
  This Hell that I call home is known as prison
So only the people that's ever been inside

Know this life and what it's like "Doin' Time"

From Me

Nothings gonna change
    It all just stays the same

Tomorrows on the way
    So I try and hide my face

Cause there's hidden darkness
    Its making me heartless

I can hardly breath
    I'm blind and cannot see

Forgive me Jesus please
    I'm down here on my knees

Can you help me one last time
    To find this soul of mine

Nothing left to give
    And sin is all I live

I can never win
    I wish this would just end

So what must I do
    I wish someone knew

Nothing left to say

        My life has slipped away
              "FROM ME"

The crazy thing is I do not remember writing this poem at all but I found it and it was halfway written so I finished it and I thought it was pretty cool and fit a tale about addiction and being hooked by the Dragon

"Dragon"

Every time I try
To kick this demon that's around me
He Breathes his fire and my desire surrounds me
He won't let me be
This crushing weight
It's suffocating me

I didn't imagine this dragon could would wreak havoc with such tragic madness but it happened indeed

This dragon's chasing me
Crisping my skin under his fiery breath
This dragon has completely charred me there's nothing left
I'm just another prisoner in his horde
Please, please help me break free

The scales on his tale shimmer and swell
Gripping and ripping as I'm drifting through Hell
Shackled by his embrace he snarls in my face
Breathing and seething I'm squeezing these chains
This Dragon has killed this crippled man
When was it that this affair began?
Cause this dragon doesn't care, I'll never be freed
He just wants to watch as I plead and bleed

This will always be one of my most favorite poems. I wrote this while I was in prison and was entered into a poetry contest. This was my first presented poem and first time I really let anyone hear my stuff. I ended up winning first place not only this particular talent shows but every one after that. Which led to me believing that maybe my poetry wasn't that bad. The purpose and message behind this poem was because due to the poetry contest we were given a list of certain topics. Ambition, Criticism, Prison, Morales, Society, World News, or Drive. We were supposed to pick one but me being me I correlated every topic into one poem.

"Driven By Ambition"

As you look around this room at all these dudes what would you conclude?

Did you base your assumption off the words that I use, the way that I move or the group that I choose to call my crew. I'm confused, maybe you think that I have a few screws loose but that's no new news cause I refuse to lose. Was your judgment just something I had coming or just an excuse? Is the difference in our pigment the reason we aint cool, or maybe I'm crazy or is it cause my tattoos? I think the racial slurs and words dispersed are really coming from you. Are you afraid to relate just in case your pride might get bruised? Or could it be you're just consumed by a bad attitude? You ever thought that me and you might have walked in the same shoes, so you shouldn't judge me and I wouldn't judge you, and it's safe to say it's never ok to only assume.

You and I are not so different, for instance, look at where were sittin. Have You used or used to count the sales off the scales as a way of livin, or maybe even been into pimpin women, knew someone close to you who died in an instant. Have you lied or witnessed hard times that led to the crimes committed. Not to mention all the victims due to our decisions, deep down those were never my intentions. You ever watch your Mother be beaten senseless, cause you was too little and defenseless to stop the relentless whippins, so you would just hide and cry in the kitchen, and sit and listen to her scream from the obscene abuse she was getting. Have you ever tired suicide cause something was missin, when you were a kid did you ever picture prison, I know I didn't but here's the difference. I'm a firm believer in never quittin just ask my addiction and in the same sense that last sentence was written I've have enough so let's discuss somethin positive for a minute. The motivation and determination and reasons why I'm driven it's not a contradiction it's a little gift I've been given that's called ambition.

I try not to focus on the hopeless emotions, but this hocus pocus potion is a notion that I've chosen. And since you keep pinchin and pokin, it's time for this encryption to be decoded. So although I'm eroding & slowly decomposing, I'm frozen cause I'm the coldest at writin poems. And in a moment's notice I can compose the grossest and most atrocious, unholy and ferocious, it's an ongoing mitosis that makes your liver quiver with cirrhosis. It's an openly chosen psychosis growing in the ocean that comes in waves and leaves you broken, speechlessly unspoken, shocked and never knowin if it's real or I'm just jokin. I'm not finished my ambition should be duly noted. It's a galactic cosmoses, a compacted osmosis that got shot in your soul like you got holy ghosted. I'm like a pit bull whose mouth is foamin. A rollin stone who's too cold to ever quit roamin. There's no need to keep this goin, I'm the master of my craft yeah I'm the poet it's not supposed. And judgin by the lack of laughs and how my omnipotence is showin, I think you know it.

Humble I may seem, but please do not compete, cause I'm so hungry when I eat, and I'm a beast when I feast. Even the Chinese make believe pre-conceived disease Covid-19 couldn't beat me, cause I'll never accept defeat. My poetry's deep, it flows so freely and easily it's a breeze, there's no levels to my degree. I'm so distinct and unique cause I critique and tweak each piece with my own technique. Now if you'll excuse me while I get serious with this speech, as we pay homage to those deceased while our people in the streets, stand and scream and rightfully fight and protest the police. For people like George Floyd may he rest in peace. So let's take a moment of silence, and in his memory we will breathe.

Ok back before you can leave, matter of fact it's hard to perceive, the way I say things with such speed I'm a freak, and I can have you weak on your feet, as I grab you and have you on the edge on your seat. It's like you're on the go and trying to fall asleep, your dreams a reality and normality's make believe. I'm a curse that gets worse, you can't teach or reach what you don't see. I make stories come to life when I write on these sheets, as it seeps and leaks in these heaps of a mystique master piece. My blood flows through my pen so I bleed with the ink.

Alright. I'm past my limit, the mask is lifted, and my contrast is exquisite to the task that's been given. You know how fast that was written, how vast and quick witted I am when against the opposition. I can outlast the competition, even when I'm only half committed. Sorry bout that but I had to brag for a minute, on my extravagant intuition, and my immaculate composition, no need to say it I already did it. So let's get back on track now that I have your attention, don't ask just listen, don't laugh I'm ventin or I'll be drastically livid. Look at all the consequences from all our bad decisions, look around you isn't this a vivid enough description? But we can bounce back in an instant, so we never have to come back to prison, but we have to act different, no more addin grams and half's to digies, as you're practicing the addition to your addiction like a bad mathematician. And trust me I get it, it's not that simplicit, but if you forget the gimmicks and stop pretendin, believe and maybe even lean on religion, you can get out of this system. And then life might be worth livin, have faith in yourself have a positive vision, take a new road, go home, and be Driven By Ambition!

From Me is a song I wrote that is a cry out for help. Someone searching for answers and never anyone around to help find truth or answers.

"FROM ME"

Nothings gonna change
        It all just stays the same

Tomorrows on the way
        So I try and hide my face

Cause there's hidden marksmen
        And my visions darkens

I can hardly breath
        I'm blind and cannot see

Forgive me Jesus please
        I'm down here on my knees

Can you help me one last time
        To find this soul of mine

Nothing left to give
        And sin is all I live

I can never win
        I wish this would just end

So what must I do
        I wish someone knew

Nothing left to say
My life has slipped away
"FROM ME"

Another love poem and every single word I have ever written is all original not once have I ever ripped anything from anyone I wrote this poem years ago way before Blake Shelton wrote his song "God Gave Me You" there's no way I can really prove this other than to say there is a lot more artist and better songs I would have ripped from than just this one so this is my version and I hope you like it.

God Gave Me You

Every day I lie awake thinkin' of how I should say it
And every night I try by closin' my eyes and prayin'
That I'll be released to my soulmate when they open the gate you'll be waitin'
And I'm grateful that "God Gave Me You", along with patience

I'm so in love with you that there's just no words
You're a want that I need so bad that it hurts
An image of perfection that I don't deserve
But "God Gave Me You" out of everyone on earth

Your beauty can write the laws of attraction
Just a simple smile can be such a distraction
And the slightest touch has such a reaction
"God Gave Me You" cause he knew it was true passion

You never lose sight no matter how rough
My ride or die my all white dove
Always by my side when times get tough
And "God Gave Me You" so we both could find love

I'm mesmerized by the way you look in my eyes
Dazed by the way you complete my life
Amazed every day you let me call you mine
And "God Gave Me You" until the end of time

"God Gave Me You" cause I was a disaster

"God Gave Me You" cause you heal me with your laughter

"God Gave Me You" so we can write a new chapter

"God Gave Me You" and that's all that matters

"God Gave Me You" so we can live happily ever after

This is a very deep song I wrote saying my final goodbyes to a dear friend who lost his battle to addiction and this goes out to anyone who has ever lost someone.

"Goodbye"

Verse 1-   Farewell my friend, 'till we meet again
           Wish I could take your place
           How I miss the smile, on your face
           You look so peaceful
           Overlooking your casket, take me instead
           This life you can have it
           Wish I could take my last breath
           Inside as you rise, from the dead

Pre-Chorus-   Please, watch over me
              Please, watch over me

Chorus=   I say my goodbyes
          Wipe the tears from my eyes
          This is not the end my friend but goodbye

Bridge-   La, La, La, La, La

Pre-Chorus-   Please watch over me, Please, watch over me

Chorus-   I say my goodbyes
          Wipe the tears from my eyes
          This is not the end my friend but goodbye

Outro-   Goodbye

A daunting tale about a acid trip and the motions along the crazy roller coaster ride of the trip I wanted to write a poem as crazy as I could make it about the throes of LSD.

I Just Did Cid

I can't hide from this monster
Even under my cover
I'm seeing sound and hearing color
Wait I said that wrong it's way too profound
I meant to say I'm hearing color and seeing sound

Sheets of LsD and Adderall
the dragon crawl
My mind rings but I can't answer that call
Breathing walls
Red waterfalls
Bouncing astounding clowning, Frowning balls

Watching the rotation of the fan
Out pops spiderman
Driving supermans van
Too scared to move I don't think that I can
Some suggests if I had legs I should have ran

Watching a leprechaun spawn right through the door
Dripping gold all over my floor
I dropped too much acid that's for sure
My jaw is raw getting' sore
That scary fairy larry shouldn't have given me more

Now I'm freezin'
ceilin shrinkin'
Is that me squeakin' as I'm breathin'
I can hear myself thinkin'
Have to remind myself just to keep blinkin'

Crystal visuals of me tweakin'
I have to come down and stop this geekin'

Fuck this rage
Forgot my age
Putrid muck has me stuck inside this cage

Fuck it then
I'll never end
this love affair with the cid

My wrists are wide, my eyes are tied
Wait that's backwards too or did I say that right
Drooling now my mind is fried
Fooling around for the rest the night

Fantastic phantoms I cannot cope
Similar to looking inside a bright kaleidoscope
Maybe more than lsd prescribed inside that dope

No nicotine, codeine, or lean
Gemson seeds and crimson trees
Weed indeed magazines is all I read
Trip is what I eat and need

As a newborn adult or a full grown kid
As backwards as I am and as fucked up as him is
I'll say this again as I once did
I'll never end my love affair with CID

I wrote this next poem while I was in prison and had no idea what a huge success it was going to be. Obviously I wrote it for my mom to show her how sorry I was for all my mistakes and all the times I hurt her from my choices in life and when I come home and started my career as a writer and recording on Tiktok that video blew up and within a few weeks had over five thousand views so apparently people love their Mommas! I love mine too. Love You Mom

I Didn't Mean To

Misconstrusions and disillusions which led to our heads being fed with unsaid confusion
A consistent intrusion in our minds and our eyes we cry in seclusion
We're alone and cold cause the old scars and bruises

                    "I DIDN'T MEAN TO"

It was not intentional but resentful we became
Because the pain we create from everlasting mistakes
Led to unsaid frustration and hate
Making amends just tends to become mundane

                    "I DIDN'T MEAN TO"

From a nurturing degree a mother to be
Too young to conceive yet gave birth as a teen
She didn't expect to see the evil in me
But Satan indeed was her planted seed
Traded her hugs for drugs that love was his need
It's a wonder how a Mother could ever love such a fiend
I watch the tears from her eyes like a river they stream

                    "I DIDN'T MEAN TO"

She feels the sting on her very own skin
When she sees the marks and scars on his
It pierces her heart and she starts to pretend
Her world isn't dark and falling apart in the wind
But she saves her remarks as her Son lives in sin
Hiding his lies behind the mask of a grin

Wishing she could just see her own Mother again

                                         "I DIDN'T MEAN TO"

Torrents of torment deliver us now
God if you're real show me some how
Yet nothing but echoes of the silent sounds
As Lucifer's laugh on this path surrounds
And I'm standing here alone on these hollowed grounds
As her unanswered prayers are somewhere lost in the clouds

                                         "I DIDN'T MEAN TO"

Patience is practiced in places on earth
And forgiveness is given to those who deserve
Trust that is taken is forsaken and it hurts
Bridges are burning and the ashes are burnt
But the lesson I'm learning
Is that I'm her worst curse

                                         "I DIDN'T MEAN TO"

Cause I'm weak in this world to which I'm a slave
Yet I owe you my life for the breath that you gave
Memories last from the past that they came
There's few that are good cause most come with pain
You tried your best to invest in a path to be paved
But I ripped a hole in your chest from the stress that I crave

                                         "I DIDN'T MEAN TO"

Cruel intentions from a child of new
His vicious decisions sickened the mood

Demented depictions which made the news
Visits in prison become the view
As wicked partitions divided the two
You didn't raise this demon that came from you
So blame not yourself of this Hell who knew
You did all you could but no good was the use
You shouldn't love such a Son who put you through so much abuse
But I am sorry Mom because I really...

                                      "I DIDN'T MEAN TO"

I was in long term serious relationships from my past and was really in love with this woman. Granted we were young and didn't make the best choices at the time and probably were way to immature to have made our relationships last. However these woman and I shared an eternal love for one another and bond that didn't matter if we were dating or not we were still close and meant a lot to one another. Sadly, these beautiful Angels were taken from us way to soon and they all passed away and left us all heartbroken and missing them so much. I had to write something in their memory and specially to send a special letter to all these women's Children. I knew all of your mothers very personally and I knew you when you were very young. I know you hurt and you may often wonder why this happened or even be angry. I understand how you feel but I want you to know that she never wanted to leave you. None of it was your fault and I know nothing will ever bring your Mom back but you meant more to her than you will ever understand. She loved you so much, and you were the most precious thing in her life. As you get older you will come to learn that life is hard and sometimes we struggle with things that are so powerful that we feel helpless and unsure of how to overcome what we're going through. I'm sure you feel that at times when it comes to the loss of your Mom. Just know that you are strong and it will be ok. You might not be able to see her or talk to her but I promise she's with you all the time watching over you. Do your best to live your greatest life and find happiness and success make your mom proud and live for her memory you will meet her again someday. In a roundabout kind of way I look at you all as my God kids because I was there at the beginning and your mothers were truly Angels so if you ever need anything please reach out to me. I am here for you.

This poem is written in memory of the Angels we lost may you Rest in Peace I love you all...

Kayla Leidig- Aug 14, 1991-Jun 20, 2014

Andrea Brown- Feb 17, 1994-Jun 24, 2019

Shanda Spacy- Feb 11, 1991-Feb 1, 2020

Jenna Thornsberry- Oct 4, 1992-Aug 26, 2023

                Gone But Not Forgotten...

"I Fall for Angels"

Every so often we encounter those that are once in a lifetime
And their soul was whole so I made her mine
But these rare gems tend to have shortened timelines

I had a few angels that I happened to love
That came down from heaven but earth wasn't enough
So they flew back to where they came from on the wings of a dove

These women were mothers and wonders while they were here
And losing them is still hard after all these years
I can't hide my sorrow with tomorrow comes tears

They left behind this void that's broken our hearts
This world has been empty ever since their depart
So I wait to see you again as I dwell in the dark

I fell for you the first time that we met
I miss you all and I can't forget
I fall for angels but mine were laid to rest

A love poem that has somewhat of a transitional twist. To say that you get lonely with someone sounds crazy but the meaning is deep and if you pay attention as you read it then it makes sense in a deep beautiful poetic way.

I Get Lonely with You

I get lonely with you,
But not in the literal sense, this gets way more intense
There's so much that I miss, like the suspense that I get when we kiss.

Stricken with heartache, as we lie awake at night
Alone and cold, wishin' we had each other to cuddle up to tight.

Tossing and turning under the cover
Dreaming you could reach out, or shout for your lover
Just so the two of you can hold on to one another.

Your restless mind taunting you, of what the one you love is doing
The occasional whiff of their scent, haunting your memories, those you fear losing.

I miss driving or riding in the passenger seat
The simple things is what makes me miss you, and you miss me
Laying on the couch, hand in hand watching tv
Everywhere one would go, the other was sure to be
And when we're apart, our hearts start to get lonely

Even though I'm gone when that certain song comes on
We can almost hear each other singing along
"I get lonely with you" and it comes on so strong

Whatever plans we may make
Whatever kind of break we may take

It's hard to contemplate, the level of loneliness we may create
It's all for the love, and the trust that we partake

I know you get lonely, cause I get lonely too
But at least we're together, and "I get lonely with you"

Just a dark gothic love poem that came to me out of the blue as I was composing this book that I thought was catchy so I added it as last minute!

I Hate the Way That I Love You

Your imprint leaves a permanent stain
Scaring me with betrayal, inflicting pain

Sometimes we regret so often we love
Life awaiting death as the caskets covered up

Your written words need not go unspoken
Links in a chain that can never be broken

Your pictures are worth a thousand words
However I decide to surrender it always hurts

I give into doubt as I let our sorrow in
Avoiding tomorrow hoping it won't begin

My heart is scared and black always
But I take you back you steadily amaze

The beauty of love crashes to the ground
Swimming through your ashes yet still I drown

You make me this way yet I stuck through
I hate the way that I love you

This was a poem that I wrote to my addiction. How much it has taken from me how I was deceived and forsaken. What all I went through because of this terrible thing. I wanted to tell my addiction how I felt after I learned to truly hate it so I hope those of you who been through this shit or even those who don't understand the struggles and life of an addict and what we been through here is some insight.

'I HATE YOU"

"I Hate You"
For giving me life that you filled with fear
You stole my soul I didn't ask to be here

Lovable laughter plagued with disaster from the initial encounter
Karma is a bitch & the tricks that surrounds her

"I Hate You"
For the fiery desire that you sparked in my heart
It was love at first sight despite its start

I embrace your taste, a life of waste I digress
Haunting & taunting such a chaotic mess

"I Hate You"
For the things you made me miss most
It's strange to be surrounded by people yet feel so alone

Driving your spikes further through flesh
Ripping & tearing the broken heart from my chest

"I Hate You"
For the tears & the fear that my loved one's shed
It's all I can do to keep from blowing a fuckin hole in my head

So I pray every day for strength as I dig deep inside
Cause death is right around the corner I'm on the border of suicide

"I Hate You"
Cause at times & in my mind I thought you had my best interest
But you hurt me & burnt me like an estranged mistress

Using & confusing this shell that's empty
Death seems best, the dead I envy

"I Hate You"
For the oddity that's gotten me to this shallow point
Obviously it's got to be my destructive choice
But damn you for the strings that you have hold in my back
I'm forever your puppet & you love it in fact

"I Hate You"
For the times & the lies that you made true
Twisted and demented the vivid picture etched into view

The pain from your stain it won't fade through
But "I HATE YOU" most because I MADE YOU!!!

This was a love poem I wanted to write to declare my promise to the woman I love and my level of promises to her kinda corny but its sweet hope someone likes this one.

"I Promise"

I promise to be there through the good times and the bad
To have you and to hold you when you're mad and you're sad

I promise to always put you first even above myself
Cause no one can compare to you there's just no one else

I promise I won't run when times get hard
I won't break these promises; I won't break your heart

I promise not to leave when you question you and me
Cause I believe we both were destined to be

I promise to support, protect & comfort in your time of need
For you are the air in my lungs that I need to breathe

I promise this life to only us two
I promise to never give in to no one new
I promise you my heart although misused
I promise to be honest and never untrue
I promise it's no option I'll never abuse
I promise from the bottom of my heart till it's through
These are just a few of the things "I Promise You"

Throughout my many relationships the question seemed to always get asked why do I keep pushing people away and so I did what I do best and I wrote about it. Yeah you guessed it in poetic composition so these are why I pushed people away and why I am so flawed I guess and why it is so hard to love me.

I Push You Away

I push you away
Because my past is nothing but pain and sorrow
And we can't promise a future in tomorrow
I always felt you were different from the start
But every girl I ever loved ended up crushing my heart
I push you away
Since I'm programmed to have doubt and uncertainty
But it's all due to my own insecurity
I'm constantly thinking negative which puts shit in my head
It's just easier to hurt you than to be hurt by you so I push you away instead
I push you away
Because I have yet to be proven wrong
There's been so many broken promises that I've heard for so long
So don't lead me to believe in you and me if it's somethin' you don't mean
Cause I'm gonna do what I gotta do even if it means leave
I push you away
With my attitude and when times get hard
I act like I don't give a fuck and I sure can play the part
I simply don't know what it's like to have someone loyal
Betrayals all I've had in the past it's sad how it un foiled
I push you away
For all the stab wounds in my back
There's been so many that I've lost track
And when it comes to you it's not just lust
But you gotta understand it's hard for me to trust

I push you away
Because I'm really scared of you
And not for what you've done but for what you could do
With so many what "ifs" that run through my mind
Loyalty is easy to have yet hard to find
I push you away
Since it's all I know
I dip out on you before you can go
When we're mad and we fight I say hurtful things
But the guilt kills me from your tears that it brings
I push you away
Because it's easier ok
A lot less harder than when I pretend to stay
I push you away
So I won't stress everyday
Who you're talking to and what the fuck is his name
I push you away
Because I've played all these games
I push you away
Since it feels the same
I push you away
Despite how far we came
I push you away
With the purpose of pain
I push you away
And it rakes my brain
I push you away
Baby but I'm the one to blame

I Strive is just something I came up with on a whim I wanted to see how long I could drag out rhyming that same syllable I guess and continue to tell somewhat of a story that made sense.

I Strive

I search deep inside and throughout my life I've failed but tried, I've cried and lied and once or twice I've tried suicide but that time I don't like to describe why it was justified my past has to be left behind or it will always reside as a feat too high but one thing I'd like to recite is my drive to climb so high that I fly outside the lines of the sky to where no eye can find my mind or compare to mine 'cause it's so divine unlike a mime that has a hard time trying to describe his kind of rhyme he's trying to define a fairy tale line that makes you cry and liquefies your eyes such as the twine on the spine of a book you look and like yet it's worn and torn so tight and only by a thread survives the moon holds gloom but will subside so that the sun shall arise and align the sky with bright light that shines and it might invite a plight of fright to those who lose sight but when you drive your mind with the right type of high you continue to drive and climb and forget those times that you hate to describe it's a memory left behind I will let you decide did *I Strive*?

Just a love poem about a man who ruined his relationship and hurt the love of his life. How he is full of regret and pain from his mistakes. But pretty much professing his love and his apologies to the one that got away.

"I'm Sorry"

I'm sorry that I misjudged your love
    And that I treated you like you wasn't good enough.

I'm sorry that I went behind your back
    Disrespecting you I know there's areas in which I lack

I'm sorry if you felt you was just an advantage
    I know I took you for granted and perhaps had a lack of compassion

I'm sorry my past corrupted our future
    And how I threw it away for a loser

I'm sorry that I made you hurt in the first place
    I don't understand how I could create such pain

I'm sorry for my mistakes I know it's too late but I'm trying
    I only destroyed you from all my lying

I'm sorry for going against the grain
    It was all my fault my insults are to blame

I'm sorry baby I truly am
    I'm so lost without you I'm a lonely man....

Another love poem short simple and sweet.

Inside Our Dreams

It's strange the ways people become engaged
The way you meet is unique and at times deranged
When the ones you least expect to be sweet turn out to be great
It's hard to wait for the day you two can finally embrace

They say time is of the essence
But here lately I've been digressing
Cause the time we was givin' is supposed to teach us a lesson
But all its done is to lead us to depression

So I spend my lonely nights tossin' and turnin'
I think of you and one thing is for certain
Is when I stare at your picture all is perfect
Cause you're the pain relief to all of my hurtin'

So picture us together you and me
Hand in hand happy and free
And tonight as we each drift off to sleep
We can both be together inside of our dreams

This poem is very special to me because I feel like in the smallest amount of words it best describes me so it was very personal and written about me when I was at a very lonely place. I actually wrote this while staying with my father and was paranoid on a long drug bender locked inside his laundry room feeling like the only thing I had at that moment was ME!

Is Me

Sometimes I wake up, alone in the dark
Sometimes I'm afraid, of the pain in my heart

I face the mirror, and it shatters my hand
Broken inside, just a shell of a man

Time passes me as life drifts on by
I've lost it all, there's nothing left to find

The only thing that I have left, IS ME

It's hard to breath with nowhere to go
It's my final attempt, and I'll go it alone

Haunted by pain and taunted by fear
Screams from the past is all that I hear

So dig deep down and what do you see
I see myself and he is me

The only thing that I have left, IS ME

I wrote this to my perfect beautiful baby girl I have never loved like the emotions and feelings I get when I am with my Daughter. When I hold my baby girl the entire world stands still, everything around me fades away and it's just me and her. When she smiles at me the ground beneath my feet turns to clouds and I have this overwhelming flood of just purity and innocence that makes me want to stand for her and protect her from everything bad and scary anything that may hurt her or even has the possibility of creating the smallest spec of sadness for my baby girl the love I have for my princess is indescribable so this one was written to show my sweetheart how much her Daddy adores her and how thankful I am to have her I love you Isabella Raelynn Easterday, I'm always with you

"Isabella"

When I hold you, I know you feel the connection
I show you unfoldable and emotional protection
Devotional unquotable affection a hypnosis of unspoken
Negotion that's a supposed direction my love for you baby
Comes from a Fathers perspective.

Derived from time a beautiful design such precious this message
From Heavens divine perfect your eyes a smile so kind
You have given me life oh Daughter of mine

Memories well gather with healable laughter when somethings the matter I'll be With you long after my life was a mess I confess a disaster before you came Nothing could have made me happier for without you my world would up and just Shatter.

Once I looked into those blue eyes a new your face was made by God I just knew Nothing else was more important than this little girl in view I kissed your soft Head as I said how much I loved you

You couldn't imagine my madness before you came what tragic sadness and my Mishaps and shame you are pure magic that happened to change my ways I'd do Anything in this world just to take away your pain Daddy loves you ISABELLA I'll never Take your name in vein...

Daddy

Just another love poem but everyone always uses the reference of King and Queen in terms of a relationship so this one was my version of a poem doing the same thing and using it as a fairy tale castle theme so I think it was pretty cute and romantic a lot of people enjoyed this love poem.

King & Queen

It's a hassle to run a castle just ask any King
Especially without a woman that he can crown Queen
Fairy tales are real although most make believe
It's weird how she appeared almost straight from his dreams

He's ready for war when his Queens by his side
Tends to his wounds like a true ride or die
A freak in the sheets his Queen screams through the night
Her body is his as she does what her King likes

Runnin the hive till the King is free
While I'm inside she's Queen bee in the streets
She can drive the empire it's fine by me
Separated by time, but she's still mine you'll see

Broken hearts when were apart, divided we fall
Together hand in hand woman and man we stand tall
My Queens protection, her solid brick wall
And she's my affection this King has it all

Happily ever after like beauty and the beast
I wear the pants but she wears the ring
Loyalty to me is royalty to a King
And she's down as can be, and loyal is my Queen

This is a song I wrote while I was in Rehab and it means so much to me. This song could have so many meanings and be for so many people. It could be for someone who's just lost at sea trying to keep their head afloat searching for direction and it could even be referred as a relationship and the lighthouse someone needs to guide them. Plus I really love lighthouses this song has so much depth to it I think it could be a hit if someone can sing it good.

"Lighthouse"

Verse 1-   Capsized, yeah, I'm steady sinking under
Baptized by the rain and thunder
It's no surprise that's there's no one under...me

Emotions focused, but I'm lost at sea
My ocean's broken, but it flows so free
So the notion seems a hopeless...Dream

Pre-Chorus-   But there's hidden darkness
That's making me heartless

Chorus-   There's nowhere to be found, when your only sight is sound
Such a lonely cold ground when you find yourself without your
Lighthouse
Your Lighthouse

Verse 2-   Sailing through the seas yet I always sink
Drowning in the shallows of a creak so deep
Exposing all my secrets that I try to..... keep

Boat wont float it's on the ocean floor
Bobbing through the waters as I search for more
Hated by the waves that tear me..... more

Pre-Chorus- But there's hidden darkness
That's making me heartless

Chorus- There's nowhere to be found, when your only sight is sound
Such a lonely cold ground when you find yourself without your
Lighthouse

Your Lighthouse

This one I am very proud of. A lot of people have asked me to write poems for them over the years and this one in particular was meant for someone else. A good friend of mine asked if I could write him a poem for his wife that was the true definition of love and my most intricate work on a love poem with the deepest meaning and so I call this my "Panty Dropper" It's a very deep true love poem and I am truly proud of this one. Another close friend I met years later his wife had passed away and he actually used this poem and had it engraved on her headstone so it touched a lot of people.

Love Defined

Love is a word that's commonly misused
Between two people who are equally confused

Life is a journey and we sail through the stars
Floating through space searching for love like ours

It's so easy to tell someone what you want to feel
Yet it's hard to explain when that love is real

Day and night as I try to write I dig deep inside
But it becomes impossible to describe cause the words never come out right

It's like an internal eclipse that grips and won't let you go
Leaving you exposed and hopelessly open for show

Love is powerful and can be dangerous in a way
But only if you treat it as a game and continue to play

Then it can be whole and pure lighting an eternal fire that burns
But only if you both are sure to do your part and take turns

If love was easy then everyone would be doing it
And if you wasn't for me then I wouldn't be pursuing it

And rumor has it that time is of the essence
But here lately I've been second guessing that expression

Because were alone in the physical and it seems so hard
But were never apart if you feel it in your heart

Cause Hell can't keep you and Heaven can't hide you
No matter where you go I'll always find you

Love is a distorted tunnel and the blind lead the blind
And wherever were headed just know that I stand behind mine

Hearts can turn black if you let them stay broken
But our love is deeper than the deepest of oceans

It's a vivid picture of exquisite that I thought didn't exist
But your love is a precious piece of perfection that you consistently depict

You can't control who you fall in love with when it happens
Its full of twists and turns hurdles that hurts, concerns and static

But with love you can't succumb to the struggles and obstacles you face
You must suffer to conquer, good and the bad that's just fate

There's nothing you can't achieve if we believe we can
We'll battle out differences and together we'll stand

In the darkest of days and through the stormiest of weather
Those dreary clouds will pass and we'll still be together

Some of us struggle with love and the lack there of
Take away the trust and that person is just never enough

But of course you've been there for me more than anyone before
And I'll always be there for you with unconditional support

So I had to get this off my chest and express my mind
You're the love of my life and this is my "Love Defined"

This was a song I wrote and actually turned out to be very popular and successful. I really liked this one and am very proud of this one actually.

Love

There's a love so strong it can never be broken
Something more fiery than words yet it burns when spoken...

There's a love so strong it can withstand the sands of time
A feeling so long that it beautifully burdens the mind...

There's a love that is deeper than the deepest of oceans
Something so strong it can enlighten emotions...

There's a love so strong that even when wrong is perfect
Together you're better you heal the feel from the hurting...

There is a love so strong it's flawed but fearless
A love like law that's raw a progressive coherence...

There is a love so strong it can disintegrate the barriers that bind us apart
Along with the cold stones that have grown encasing our hearts...

There's a love in this world that will never wither or fall through
These words that I exert is just another way for me to say...

"I Love You"

This poem is written for me dear friends the Lengachers they are the greatest people I have ever met in my life and a true blessing from God. They came into my life when I needed them the most and admittingly I still don't deserve such wonderful people as friends but somehow they believed in me and gave me more chances that I ever should have gotten. I just wanted to do something special for them and write them their own special family poem and this is for you guys. (Don't ever eat a cake made by Nate) I Love Ya Buddy

"May This Family Thrive"

We live as we laugh
Yet we give what we have
The Lord is our sword
No more sorrows to be had

Together we are better "May This Family Thrive"
Like sheep we heard Gods divine

Time doth pass as life shall cease
As long as we have each other and Jesus
We'll have eternal peace

I wrote this love poem and wanted to really aim it in the direction of being addicted to a woman and her love and what better way than to describe that by depicting her love as being my "Medicine"

Medicine

When you were first prescribed you impaired my mind
But I kept taking you as I crossed that line
Consuming more of you slowly over time
And before I knew it I got used to it
And you became and addiction of mine

Without you I was so sick and alone
My dependency on you was no joke
Not caring if I overdosed, I kept you close
As I chose to up my dose
You drug me down like the weight of a stone
I'm your junkie honey and I don't care if no one knows

You're the remedy to my heart,
That was once dead in my chest
A vitamin or capsule a bottle or RX
A for sure cure to my achy head
I take my lady daily,
My baby's my meds

I don't lean on other women and their cheap thrills
What I need is a handful of her cause I crave her pills
And when I don't have her I get the shakes and the chills
It's tough when you're in love the withdrawals kills

She's stimulating like a calming muscle relaxer
And at times she's pure adrenaline

Making my heart beat faster
And if I refrain from her substance my life's a disaster
Yet I chase her dragon cause her highs all I'm after

I'm in love with her and she's in love with me
And I need this habit as a way to breathe
I never want it to cease or ever leave
This is a disease I want to keep and never beat

The monkey on my back is in fact irrelevant
Cause this addiction I'm inflicted with is a Heaven sent
And if I could I would just ingest the rest of it
As I inject my chest just for a test of betterment
I'm strung out on this drug because her love is "Medicine"

Another love poem I actually wrote this for someone else while we were in jail. They wanted me to do a poem for their girlfriend describing how she's always been there for him and how much they have in common like their love for shoes he specifically wanted that incorporated into the poem so that's why it's a little off and topic and out of nowhere but still a good love poem I felt I should incorporate into my book.

Meet in The Middle

We're afraid not of people but rather rejection
So we're distant from the world for our own protection

Persistence is key when communicating with me
And loyalty is law and it's all that I need

So when it comes to you, you've stayed so true
No matter the circumstance you've seen it through

We've learned to love and it's been since the start
And in return you've earned my heart

For you there is no chick I wouldn't quit
In the blink of an eye me and her wouldn't exist

And it's all for you this love that I feel
An emotional rush more than lust its real

But we're afraid of the pain and the things we may lose
Yet we relate to everything even our love for shoes

For whatever reason our timing was always off
But to make this work I wouldn't care the cost

I've thought of you so much my mind seems rusted
And so much more than just thoughts of seduction

I crave you uncontrollably you're an obsession of mine
Somewhat emotionally were connected through time

So no matter who, what, when, where, or why
You're my best friend till the end, my true ride or die

To give my heart to another woman I don't think I could
Cause you've always had my back, even when no one else would

Soldier to soldier two G's in the street
Shoulder to shoulder we stand when were weak

So pretend a perfect life with no games or riddles
Then picture me in your dreams and "We'll Meet In The Middle".

I write a lot about my addiction and what it's taken from me. All the misery and heartache and life scaring setbacks and damage I have done to not only myself but all those around me this one I wrote while I was in rehab and it was very moving to a lot of people I read it to my NA groups I facilitated and it had a huge impact on the audience. This is about my disease and what it does to an addict.

"My Brittle Disease"

Brittle the pieces so to begin
Drizzle the leaches that soak in sin
      I'll deliver such pleasure of Heavens divine
      But by the end of this tale farewell you're mine
            Demolish & polish the clean to dirt
            I'll collapse what's whole & relapse your earth
I'll batter your dreams & shatter your goals
I'll steal your life & I will kill your soul
      Devour your functions with death and destruction
      Implode with eruptions such sporadic abruptions
            Blind your path & cloud your mind
            Consume your reality another casualty of mine
Collective is he who surrenders to me
Slow or go you seem to erode with speed
      Focus emotions that dwell so dark
      Addiction is a depiction you sell with your heart
            Demonic to you platonic to thy
            Erotic to me it's neurotic to die
Inhale my taste embrace the irony
Fail to those who hail sobriety
      Scripted is my plan which is cryptic & above me
      Wicked is this addiction your sickness is lovely
            Let sovereignty escape you as I collect
      While your children are in the wilderness all alone you neglect
I crumble empires with desires, and perish the nations
I'll tear down walls & scrawl with abrasions
      You will slowly drown in the sounds I relish

It's a curse at first then worse I embellish
Over time you'll seek help so you suppose
But it's too late as you weep in the heaps of foes
A giver of gifts such love & lust just drugs to be sold
A derailment or ailment a sick that is quick a cancer that grows
Brittle as a pencil whose been sharpened to many times
Frantic to find the last edge of lead just to write one more line
Knowing you've caused all the mistakes that led to these wrongs
With no room for errors as the erasers all gone
So face that mirror & take a close look at who you see
The torment of reflection is a deception also known as my
'Brittle Disease"

So anyone that knows me on a personal level knows that I take Brotherhood very seriously especially when it comes to my blood Brother. So I wrote this one for him to its deep and meaningful and sentimental to me and my Brother.... Love You Bubby!

My Brother's Keeper

I once made a friend
So many others were pretend
His life for mine, both I'd defend

This tale I tell, may seem meaningless oh-well
I'd go in my Brother's place if he ever fell

Mixed emotions and broken dreams
Together we stand, an unbeatable team

No one can compare to my Brother I swear
Your problems are mine, our burdens we share
No one will cross us, no one shall dare

I've looked, I've searched, I've fought and bled
For a bond like ours, words spoke un-said

"My Brother's Keeper" for it's he who I knew
He'd go to war with God for me and I for him too

I give you my life, long after death
I'll stand for our brotherhood till my last breath

This poem was influenced by one of my favorite songs called "My Distorted Reflection" by Upon a Burning Body. Of course it's all my original words I just loved the title and it gave me this idea to create this story about just hating what you see and the person you have become how sick you are when you face yourself. This is one of my favorites.

"My Distorted Reflection"

Are you like me & only see, the way we lose?
When you look in the mirror who is looking back at you
Is it a real life story, is it bloody is it gory, how much is true?
A figment of your imagination, a pigment or creation, a colorful cartoon?
Because my reflection is distorted & I'm confused on what to do....

So this is it & here I stand
Tripping & gripping this pistol in my hand
Who am I, I can't understand
But all that's visible is the remanence of a broken man....

It's like watching a broke TV, just static
Suddenly & abruptly I become frantic
Mocking myself as I start to panic
Cause this image saddens me drastically
Wish I could leave it's hard to breath, like an asthmatic
And what's staring back at me, laughing is tragic....

I face myself cause no one has the heart
The road to Hell is a swell place to embark
Yet as I look close I'm not alone in the dark
Because I have me & he I cannot flee or ever depart....

While gazing upon myself, I notice that I've become quite feeble
As I try to picture myself in church, I can almost hear the people
In the distance I can see me on my knees looking up at the steeple

But then it all fades in distortion & my praying hands I'm clutching a needle....
It becomes clear as can be to me
And suddenly so visibly & vividly
I finally start to see
That I wasn't meant to be
Freely in society, the irony
Stuck in the frame of this horrid scene
Conflicted, tormented & trapped in this demented motion picture dream....

I'm so tired of playing the same fucking game
I just keep doing the same thing am I fucking insane
The color from my face starts to drain
Cause I've always looked at but now I feel the windows pane....

Although selfishly, my mind wonders helplessly
Vile tidal waves crash into me
Sailing blindly into misery reef
Like an abandoned ship lost & lonely at sea
And before I can think or blink, I sink so deep....

Watching my ego & those who bruised it
Reflecting on my life & how it's ruined
I search for meaning & purpose, understanding & translucence
And any happiness I may have found,
You could look right through it....

Scared, I don't try to be
But these insecure demons deep inside of me

Has me on the edge of this bed suicidally
Watchin time & my life pass through this glass
I'm my own worst enemy & I'm eyein me....
The voices in my head get loud
It's an annoyance but there all around
My choices have led me to be unsound
So I must destroy this mirror before it puts me in the ground....

Because I hate this place
I hate to gaze at my own face
Staring at myself, I stare back dazed
Lost in this place like I'm in a maze
It shall be said best when I'm laid to rest that I was a grotesque mess
Who couldn't change his ways....

There's no need to tell why, it's reported & suspected
I'm unwell but I tried, I was unsupported & infected
Living in Hell and this realm is the contorted section
Oh well because this is "My Distorted Reflection"

There were times when I really questioned if I was going to live or die and I pushed my limits for so long that I had no clue when my time may come so I thought it would be fitting and just make sense for me to not only write my own Eulogy but to do it the way I write best by doing it with a poem a lot of people really favor this one.

My Eulogy

We gather for this lost man's sake
Let us pray his soul the lord will take
The man who passed away is Joseph Easterday
Born in 91 the 20th day of May
Many of you have tears in your eyes, it's no surprise
But he was un-happy in this life
Hence the reason for his demise
Born to a Mother too young to show love
Would have been happy with just a hug
He craved her attention, it was never enough
So he found solace through the use of drugs
His Grandmother died right in his hands
He turned into a hopeless & broken man
So lost and sad he didn't understand
Prison became home the only place he could stand
He left behind a sign of pain
On everyone's face from the choices he made
But his debt to society has been due-fully paid
As his casket drops and his body rots
Life no more his time has stopped
He let it be known while he was here
That death was something he did not fear
But the great beyond is so unclear
Ashes to ashes and dust to dust Heaven or Hell one is a must
So I hope he found peace and someone to trust
Your funeral here was set to show, people loved you just so you know
Rest in peace wherever you go, this eulogy was wrote just for Joe.

Another Mom poem I seen my Mother go through so much shit and still manage to be this bad ass that takes on everyone's problems and still can maintain her own life she's had a lot of heartache and disappointment setbacks and misery loss and sorrow but still keeps it all together and stays strong for all of us so this was just me paying homage to her and all her strength.

My Mother's Strength

A strong woman will often feel miserable
For her own reasons, I guess its sacrificial
Even with a son on the run who's forever criminal
My mother, I love her she's so strong and invincible

Stress level so high she can hardly think
With having her accounts all drained at the bank
Credit cards maxed she gets taxed to the brink
I don't know how my mother can recover such uncanny strength
But somehow she discovers this love for others and it has no length

Life is short and then we die
And just the thought of losing you kills me inside
But I promise to do better I swear I'm gonna try
And the next time that I ever see you cry
I hope its cause I made you proud from the loud tears in your eyes

She's constantly stressed she's cursed yet blessed
And she often complains about pain in her chest
Every days a test I just wish she would rest

Working harder than anyone to only earn pain
And all the men in her life are both one in the same
I wish she knew how sorry I was because I'm part of the blame
As to why she has to fight just to see the sunshine through the rain

She's earned the right to be suspicious of people's intentions

She always listens to everyone's problem's and bad decisions
They show up broke and in hopes that she can fix it
What worthless fake and fictitious idiots they're so senseless
Preying on my Mother cause she's a Christian it's endless
Selfish and relentless it sickens me when wicked people use religion
Leaving people like her bleeding cause their needing attention
Not to mention all the criticism she's getting cause her kids sittin in prison
It's like she's doing the time but her misery is her sentence

I can't comprehend how she can have any forgiveness
Yet she does and it's so tremendous
She never needed a man she has her own independence
My mom's my hero and her strengths the biggest
She comforts me through the phone, with letters and visits

She has the heart of a lion yet she's soft to the touch
And everyone leans on her using her as crutch
Holding their hands out expecting so much
She takes the weight of the world and she don't even hunch

My Mom can handle more than God can withstand
She's my inspiration a one woman band
And I owe it to her to become a better man
Where my Mother gets her strength I'll never understand

This poem is a sentiment of how a man can just wonder through life lost and stuck in the shadows. How depression and addiction can consume you and you just never find your way back. A portal to nowhere and the journey you face along the way. I wrote this during one of my prison bits I can't remember when or where I was I just know I was locked up and feeling this way in my own mind.

My Own Maze

So cold I can see my breath
I knew right yet I chose left
So this path I must accept
Its lead to a new depth
And next must be death...
I push on as I sulk
In circles as I walk
Voices seem to talk
Through this journey I embark
But its only me, alone in the dark...
There's no sense of time
Lost sight plus my mind
Both I may never find
Or my way to the other side...
This roads so fuckin long
When you walk it all alone
Everyone has gone
So hatred comes on strong
The betrayal feels so wrong...
Traveling endlessly
Carrying misery
And painful memories
But there my own and it gets to me
Relentlessly so much that it's all I see...
All those freaks that I meet
Leaves scars and bruises on my feet
Snakes are discrete, take and they cheat

Making you incomplete
They lie and deceive, try and they succeed...
Lost and confused
On which way I should choose
Drugs I abuse
And these tracks I'll never lose...
Stuck in my own ways
Wondering around for days
This pain won't go away
Trapped in "<u>My Own Maze</u>"

This was written for another buddy of mine dedicated to his wife. He asked me to do something special for their anniversary basically expressing his true love for her. A confession of his flaws mistakes and areas he lacks and should improve in. Basically an apology of poetic proportion.

My True Love for You

I never listen or pay attention to your problems or business
I'm usually too busy with my own bullshit & gimmicks
And the sickest part is that my heart is so relentless at makin' decisions
It took me a minute to admit but I've come to my senses
I'm dyin' for your forgiveness and I'm tryin' to fix this
Lyin' when I say I don't miss your hugs and kisses and how much I hate the distance in us
I'd change it all in the flip of a switch in just an instant
For just a pinch of your repentance or just an inch of innocence

Of course I'm regrettin' gettin' arrested so this issue
I'm pressin' and steadily addressin'
Is a confession off my chest of all my sins and deception
So I'm sorry for all the negative aggression it was a neglective infection

That led to me constantly disrespectin' you
Yet I'm possessive and obsessive over you
But what else are you expectin' boo
Cause you're the closest thing to heaven that I ever knew

So wipe off that blank expression make an exception, stop stressin' and second guessin'
I've learned my lesson answer my question: what else can I do?

Other than apologize for the emotional abuse I put you through there's no excuse

For all the lies that I tried to use as a ruse to confuse you
So I could do what I do, I broke your heart we drifted apart and I didn't mean to
And for the first time in my life I'm telling you the truth

I want to change the mistake that I've made that caused heartache and hate
That left a bitter taste in your face that's so hard to erase
I'm pouring my heart out in hopes that it won't leave a permanent stain
I just wish I could have replaced the crosshairs of aim and distain
So you wasn't the target left bleeding scarlet with pain

A relationship is unique when you each meet and we as a team have our own distinct technique
A certain mystique so to speak you may argue and disagree but over time critique and tweak
His and her needs which brings you each peace and a sense of relief
So husband and wife can coincide and find ease
So please, just breath, don't leave and when you think of me don't compare me to a disease
I know it ain't easy to please me, believe me, and I don't mean to seem cheesy
But you need me and I need you I'm needy and when it comes to you I'm greedy
I took for granted all your decency and recently
I've been screamin' in my dreams
Pleadin' just for you to speak to me

So with these words that I wrote I spoke the truth
I promise to change and I mean it too

It's a given I'd give my life but I want to live for my boo
There's nothin' in this world that I wouldn't do
Just to prove <u>My True Love For You</u>

This one I actually wrote for a friend of mine who wanted me to write a poem for his Father and what he meant and he was specific on all the details he wanted included. My Pops was still living at the time I wrote this and it wasn't until years later after mine passed and I re-read this poem did it really hit home and I couldn't believe how similar it was to me and my Father's relationship. I miss him so much and think about you every day Pops I hope your tearing those streets of Gold up on your Heavenly Harley.

Never Forget You

I came into this world lookin' for answers
You made my bottles and changed my pampers
Hide and seek you'd find me in the hampers
On vacation sleepin' in campers

My birthday parties I sure do miss
Blow out my candles, you'd say make a wish
I'll never forget you taught me to fish

You'd walk me through the dark holdin' my hand
We'd play catch and wrestle in the sand
You sacrificed so much, did all that you can
You're my hero and I'm your biggest fan
I'd be nothing without my ole man

You instilled in me to be all I can be
Live your life boy, be better than me
But when I picture greatness, it's you I see

I close my eyes and think of those nights
Of us in the drive, teachin' me to ride my bike
Hit harder and faster if you wanna win a fight
Mom would get mad, but you'd make it alright
But I want to say thank you Dad, I owe you my life

As I got older and I got a chip on my shoulder
My mind started to wonder, my heart grew colder

I would only change our past
Just to make it last
My time with you flew too fast

You and Ma used to pray till your knees gave way
Done more than enough that's safe to say
Seeing your disappointment used to make my heart break
But I never meant to hurt you, I'm so sorry for my mistakes
And I'll see you again one of these days
Never feel guilty or like you failed
Because your fatherly love is what prevailed

I can never thank you quite enough
Even for the love that was tough

Don't blame yourself or hold your breath, even though you taught me right I still found left
And I'm gonna continue to fuck up till my death

You're the best Dad that I ever knew
Nothing in this world my pops couldn't do
We'd get it in and screw bitches to
I miss you old man I'll never forget you

This one is just a biography basically written about me and my feeling about my life what I been through and at the time of my life I was at everything was dark and gloomy so I was suffering in my own seclusions.

"Nothing Left"

We battle our demons one fight at a time
But the victories iffy cause it's not always mine

Standing steady and I'm already sore
Cause the weight is heavy when you're not ready for war

It's easy to lose sight of our common goal
Cause the road can be cold when you walk alone

Shell shocked as the moment's lapse
Tick tock as the clocks collapse

There's "Nothing Left" I've lost it all
It slipped away the day that I fell off

It comes in waves like a hurricane
Pleasure and pain are like pressured rain

Curled in a ball as I fall from joy
The sounds profound it's like quiet noise

I drift away as the days they sink
I'm in too deep and my thoughts won't sleep

I swallow my pride as I follow my death
Hollow inside because there's "Nothing Left"

This is very dark and could even be misinterpreted as an evil poem. But before you judge it and take it as that hear my reasoning and purpose behind it. So I wrote this poem not in a sinister wicked way or to praise the devil but the purpose of this poem is to shed light on the wicked ways of the world and just the evil that we actually live in how blind we are and how easily it is for us to fall victim to denouncing God as our lord and savior and just how caught up we get into the ways of the devil and how intrigued we can become when we become frustrated with God and our understanding of him.

Oh Faceless One

<u>Oh Faceless one</u>: please sit with me, tell me a tail and vent to me
Make it dark and interesting, I had this epiphany that you would be sent to me
Is the underworld sacred and menacing
Do demons sing like in symphony
Tell me some secrets that no one knows
And what happens after we decompose
Do we drift off into darkness, is that where our soul goes
And how much will you give for mine for the right price it can be sold

<u>Oh Faceless one</u>: what is past the sun
When has our journey officially begun is there a place to run
Being wicked is fun
Or must we only die and fry under the evil eye of an evil nun
I feel your presence strong and in essence it don't feel wrong
So take me to your dark synagogue and make your blasphemous sermon long
As you lead me astray from that old waste of space faith
To which I prayed for days
On my hands and knees begging please to a God who only pushed me away

<u>Oh Faceless one</u>: show me the answers I seek
I fear not the wisdom and truth you speak
Wandering so long, lost and gone screaming till I was weak
For my time to pass in such a flash memories are so bleak

Oh Faceless one: somehow come down to my low life level
And let's revel in this headful of sin it's sick and oh so dreadful
Then let's begin as you enter in
This world that's ruled by the devil

So another dark one but I wrote this one again NOT giving praise or glorifying anything evil someone just asked me if I could write a poem about a group of friends who sat down and played with a Ouija Board and so this was my creation. I would highly recommend to NOT mess with that stuff because you are tampering with spirits and unholy things that could hurt you and you never know the spiritual world and what your inviting into your home and or your life just be careful.

Ouija Board

Full Moon, Bright night
Red candle, Dim light
Gather Round, Clear mind
Some fear, No fright
Grab hands, Hold tight
Deep breath, closed eyes
Repeat, Recite

Séance, Open portal
Undead, immortal
Pure Dread, Not Normal
Death Bed, informal

Dark Shroud umbrella
Touch now planchette
This sin vendetta

Ask if you dare
Be afraid, Be scared
Feel faint, Cool air
A gust in your hair

Go slow it works best
Speak now confess
Seek truth, Don't stress
It don't sleep, It won't rest

Pray for your Lord
His shield, His sword
Beware, Be sure
When you end, Closed door
Take heed, it's the Ouija Board!

This is one of my all-time favorite poems and everyone who has ever heard it was just mind blown they loved it because so many people have felt like an Outcast in their life and I even changed the spelling because I felt so odd and displaced in this world at times this poem describes me so perfect and I love this one to the core I hope you do to.

Outkast

If you can't understand a man or why his heads so low
Maybe you shouldn't stare and glare let alone throw stones
    People laugh and it hurts and what's worse is I hear
    The giggles and whispers they all sound so clear
As the hours go by the torment out last
That results from the insults towards this old **"OUTKAST"**
    Ridicule is fuel and burns with a rage
    I'm in my own head and I'm alone in this cage
Paranoia can destroy ya while inducing the pain
Mortified inside but it's by my own shame
    Etched in my chest is the "S" that I scrawl
    My emotions are hopeless because I can't do it all
So point if you must and laugh as you pass
Ha-ha. He-he it's me the crazy **"OUTKAST"**
    I give too much and receive too little
    Yet you're still puzzled by this impossible riddle
I'm unique inside distinct but hallow
Cause even my own shadow refuses to follow
    But I choose to be alone not because I'm forced
    It's better that way then stay with remorse
People can lie, fake, and pretend
But only I can decide who I let in
    Memories are forever and together they last
    Alone with the curse of being the **"OUTKAST"**
I'm fragile sometimes I have feelings too
So who am I? I'm just human like you
    I keep to myself as I yell but silently

But my screams only seems to ring deep inside of me
I talk to myself when no one is around
And at times I walk with my head held down
    It's to avoid ideocracy that people portray
    Constant democracy is an annoying array
It keeps me on my toes so I can search better
Laugh all you'd like I'll be the first to find treasure
    Different in my own way even awkward perhaps
    What can I say I'm just an **"OUTKAST"**
To explain the fidgets and facial twitches
Even computers often come with some glitches
    Weird I may be to those who seem strange
    Yet normal is he who refuses to change
So single me out and call me odd
You may say that I'm off yet I think that I'm not
    Cause your knowledge is choppy and your ego is brittle
    So chime in all you'd like and you might make a symbol
Cause if I'm by myself there's no need to fret
Because only the lonely forget regret
    My silent sounds that's left with right
    I'm upside down but I found what's mine
So count your blessings and count your cash
But count me out cause I'm the **"OUTKAST"**
    I'm bullet proof so shoot and aim
    Take your shots cause I crave the pain
I may be a victim of mainstream society
Or maybe I suffer from social anxiety
    I simply don't fit in with large crowds
    My anxiety kicks in and it ripples the sound

So this is me take it or leave it
I'm as weird as it gets and you better believe it
    But people still love me for the way that I am
    I don't explain myself because you won't understand
I'm genuine and friendly honest and true
Intellectual and funny but a little off too
    So look at this face because it's not a mask
    Behind both sides lies the real **"OUTKAST"**

"Overcome" means just what it says this poem describes some of the things I've conquered throughout my life and the demons I fought with but also I wrote it from a perspective that anyone can relate to and see through their eyes as well.

"Overcome"

We fought through the mud and got drug through the trenches...
Overcome being stuck on drugs and sleeping on benches...

Brutality and sadness that some can't imagine...
Yet the strong stay alive and manage to survive the madness...

Sorrow no one knows, collect calls on those phones...
Counting down the calendars until we can go home...

If it wasn't for God we would be so alone...
We overcome our struggles and tussled with our demons...
And we changed who we was because it was needed...
We owe it all to the lord his sword was our beacon

I wrote this from a depressed state of mind and just wanted to express how real pain was and how real MY pain was so this was what I came up with

Pain So Real

Guilt spread lies

        Twisted shadows that scream inside

It's all the same "Pain So Real"

        Wounds that gape, they never heal

Silent sounds, shallow drowns,

        Drift with me on hallowed ground

Alone I stray through clouds of gray'

        Yet to find a better way

I choose to collapse & I refuse to kneel,

        Down on my knees cause the "Pains So Real"

This was a poem I wrote for Black History while I was in prison.

It was everyone by this time had gotten to hear some of my poems and so I was approached to do something for Black History Month and I'd say I killed it this should be an international poem spoken all over for The entire month of Black History I really enjoy performing this one because it catches a lot of people's attention.

"People Are Equal"

We as a people need to be treated equal we don't need a repeat or a sequel
Of all the evil we've seen amongst our people
The hatred created by those bleak, weak, and feeble

Nothings blacker than the slave traffic of Africa, so sudden and drastic
So dark and tragic we can't imagine the madness and sadness that happened
The simple fact that someone could have such a lack of compassion
And just sat back laughin as the chains were rattlin
Then men rose and there were those who chose to no longer have it
And stand up and fight for the rights of the trapped black African

So with these words spoke I hope someone will listen to me
As we pay homage to our black history by remembering
That the same misery still existed not so distantly and indiscriminately
It was still seen so vividly it sickens me

Although it was slow the slave trade faded yet for decades they still faced hatred
And found ways to maintain by being discriminated straight to their faces
And places that to this day are still complacent at being racist

We lost some greats like Malcom X and MLK so let's give thanks and appreciate The sacrifices they made even with all the criticism they had to take
So you and I can live lives as black and white as they tried to stop the hate
Rest in peace George Floyd your final breath made us awake
And we'll savor Breonna Taylor as we forever say her name

No matter your age, race, color, or creed
What God you pray to or the secrets you keep
Racism is a plague it's a deadly disease
And these are easily the reasons we need to believe so we can achieve
People are equal and we each have the right to be free

I have struggled with addiction for most of my life. I have seen death I have died myself and just watched entire cities crippled with addiction especially from prescription pills. My addiction actually was started by an injury and a Doctor feeding me pain pills. So this poem was really meaningful and personal to me. Its written from my real life stories and experiences with my addiction to pain pills.

Pills Kills

Why do I keep doing this time and time again?
Why have I lost all my family and all my friends?
Why does everyone continue to lie and pretend?
Is there any way that I can make this end?
Or is my only direction a downward descend?

The answers to these questions lie within
But not inside of me, there in a bottle you see
Purchased for cheap and found easily on the street
Through deception they stole your soul they keep
For all eternity in Hell you sleep

It started with one from one to two
You matching me and me matching you
Next thing you knew a few wouldn't do
Robbing pharmacies hardly got me through

All different colors and all different shapes

Some green like weed or purple like grapes
Not realizing the damage you manage to make
Yet we can't wait to make more of these mistakes
We still crave their taste even with all that's at stake
Once hooked on this bait you seal your fate
But by then it's way too late

Next thing you know, you're shooting up

Or its slowly going up your nose
Trading off your own kids clothes
You're broke and everyone knows
You yourself or someone you know ends up comatose
As they go through and overdose
Having to be cremated cause there so decomposed
It's gross but that's how it goes I suppose

One time my friend and I got a bunch
And we each took too much
And when I woke up he was cold to the touch
His shirt was covered from where he smothered,
On his own throw up

So I sat and cried cause my friend had died
All because he tried those pills of mine
So I hugged him, told him I loved him for the last time

Maybe these words don't hurt from the stories I tell
Maybe you don't know this life
Or ever been at the bottom of a well
Maybe if we switched lives,
Then I wouldn't be compelled
To warn you that **<u>"PILLS KILLS"</u>** so welcome to Hell.

There is really no excuse for this poem. I wanted to created this dark and twisted and crazy story about a man who was a psychopath and so I thought about if a psycho had a diary what would be in it and how I could turn that into a poetic story. This was just me being creative nothing literal or factual so please don't judge the rest of my work.

Psychopaths Diary

I only have a little bit of time left
So I scribe on these lines with my breath
Carved in my book is where they go
Dark secrets of my life no one knows

                All this sacrament
                      It don't make sense
                Trapped behind a black hole
                      Close mind, empty soul
                Binded by killing sprees
                      Blinded I cannot see
                These outrageous places
                      Makes us suicide contagious

The voices inside of me
        Breath irony
Demons scream silently
        Violently
It's a psychopath's diary
        Diary!

                I didn't mean to hurt her
                      But I love murder
                Take me to face my rage
                      Leave me inside a cage
                I'm so fuckin delirious, mysterious
                      Sounds like they're hearing us

So strap me down tightly, I'm fighting
But you'll never stop the writing
In my diary...

The voices inside of me
  Breath irony
Demons scream silently
  Violently
It's a psychopaths diary
  Diary!

This poem is really subliminal I guess it's written about voices in someone's head. Sounds that never leave or stop and just drive him to the point of insanity. Causing him to inflict self-harm just to make it all stop. I really like this poem and to make it even more unique and my own work I purposely spelled Noise wrong.

Quiet Noize

The quiet noize is what's keepin' me from sleepin'
An eerie echo of nothing like a loud crowd of quiet screamin'
Yet somehow this silent sound has my ears ringin'
Like an evil choir in a demonic church that you heard singin'

Sometimes I feel so distant as I fall apart
Cause the decibel is unquestionable it left a level mark
Well-rounded and stable like a table that cradles a harp
Like a lonely shark left alone in the dark
Or the howl of a dog his song is a bark
It's dead and & alive like a pulse with no heart

This quiet noize has me question my mental state
At this rate I feel defeated, un-needed for fucks sake
I'm drained from my mistakes I'm weakened

My souls at stake, hungry for me to feed it
Bible beside the pile of brochures to treatment
And like the cobwebs on the good book I'll look but won't read it
I've folded my hands after the man began preachin'

Beggin' for help not wealth, money can't buy what's needed
I pray for silence as the violence creeps in
The preacher's voice are whispers of lies that I try to believe in

But the quiet noize is a choice that won't escape reason
I can't take this quiet noize anymore I need treated

Like a mal nourished plant that can't be reseeded
Back against the wall as I claw at the screechin'
I climb but I fall no one at all to take my hand that's reachin'
Torn and bleedin' this scorn of interruption is an abruption not leavin'
the quiet noize is a whore that was born for deceivin'
forcing her annoyance like a flamboyant feedin'
as she toys with my breathin' with buoyant secretin'
But this fucking sound is so profound it won't cease its existence or persistence in repeatin'

I remember a world when I had a glimpse of some sanity
Where I escape the quiet noize I'm no longer a casualty
A place of purpose where quiet noize was falsie
No more gruesome sounds that surround reality
My life is alright and my mind acting rationally

Then I snap back like elastic to sporadic misery
Only this time it's to a comforting pain that I can no longer see
I gouged out my eyes and ears with sheers as they rupture and bleed
Givin' up everything around for the sounds to cease
I even sacrifice my eyes so that I am no longer naive

The mixtape melody will never be beat
It's a defining symphony that won't leave me be
And now I'm seeing this disruption like the ocean climbs the beach
As the quiet noize continues to play silently in the breeze…

This one was just a simple tale of heartbreak almost from a suicidal point of view. I got the idea one day from the very sting of love. How it can cut you and leave you with scars. What can cut? A knife or blade or a Razor then the idea just blossomed into me incorporating the story line about love being the edge of the blade itself it's pretty, shinning, looks captivating, and lures you in only to hurt you in the end.

Razors Edge

I'm so low, below the grounds above me
Seems to be that you never loved me

                        Drowning my pain with the dope that I shoot
                        You tore my heart out right down to the root

But I embrace your hate, I love the feel
Of your old blade and its cold steel

                        Maybe I'm insane addicted to pain
                        Or maybe I'll blow it away like Kurt Cobain

This road I'm on just has no end
I'm alone all the time at a steady descend

                        I crave your attention as if it were my only need
                        So I slit my wrist as I drift and watch it bleed

Your stabbing pain I felt inside of me
You severed my veins as you slept beside me

                        I can't keep my hands off you I hold you too much
                        I love the curvy edges, of your sharp touch

You're in my pocket, a locket of my body and soul
But it's been sold so I must pay the toll

Dead inside as I died on the edge of this bed
My love killed me with her "Razors Edge"

I always have been fascinated by homophones (each of two or more words having the same pronunciation but different meanings, origins, or spelling.) So I set out to write me a poem its super short but sometimes the really short stories tell the biggest tales.

"Reel Eyes"

We take a look at life as we *"Realize"* what's left

But what I *"Reel Eyes"* is that my *"Real Lies"* is defined by my own breath

Yet it's by design that I *"Realis"* my mind is the cause & effect.

So it's no surprise that in my demise my *"Real Eyes"* has primed my death!

I was angry at an ex of mine and wanted to write a twisted dark love poem about killing her and so I ripped the classic "Roses Are Red" and made it my own.

"Roses Are Dead"

Your nose is dripping red, your lips are blue
Your eyes are black & swelled shut to
Colorfully bruised like temporary tattoos
Your blood stains are splattered all around the room
Started as crimson yet it dries maroon

                        Your love was fake like an off white opaque
                        Now you look white as color drains from your face
                        Like a rotten bouquet wilted in a vase

Flowers grow & decompose, together side by side
You & him can grow together as your swarmed by flies
Ashes to ashes you both shall die

                        Roses are red violets are blue
                        Tulips lie & yours do to
                        I got nosy instead & caught you boo
                        Cozy in my bed with another dude
                        "Roses Are Dead' bitch and so are you

This poem is hard for me but so deep. I wrote this because of my struggles with not just addiction but also the needle. The needle in itself becomes another addiction of its own one that is an evil I wouldn't wish on my worst enemy. It grips the very core of your soul and so I needed to capture in my best depiction a story that would grab the reader and make them understand how deadly and destructive that syringe had been for me. I used to look down on people who shot up and swore I never would become that. I will never forget the haunting words that were said to me by the person who first put a needle into my arm. He said "Five minutes from now, you're going to love me I'll be like a God to you. But Five years from now you will hate me and I will be become the Devil you wish you never encountered". His words will forever haunt me.

Russian Roulette

That tense moment, when you hold it, sweatin, not knowin
If this will be the last time you grope this hopeless and soulless component
Its contents are potent, and the two of you are fully loaded
The likelihood of death is constantly growin from this gun that your holdin
It's still smokin, and through your veins the bullets are flowin
Straight to your heart is where there goin to explode it or slow it
To the point that the valves won't open, your steady gaspin and choking
As your lying there dying from overdosing already decomposing
You let the evil needle be the spokesman of this fatal game
Of "Russian Roulette" that you have chosen…

The weapon of choice, a single shot hundred unit, silver tip the tubes translucent
The barrel is full of fluid, the shot pattern is bruised but congruent
As you watch your blood mix in it you can see through it
Packing a punch but not a bunch of movement, its fluent
Brand new or used we still abuse this nuisance
But when you fire it, your ears ring with music
That's beautifully amusing…

Every time you pull the trigger, your eyes dilate twice in size and are inclined to get bigger
It takes your breath, you clutch your chest as your heart beat gets quicker
Your teeth chatter, somethings a matter, your vision flickers

Hair stands up, can't speak up, only whisper some sort of gibberish
The syringe had his revenge the almighty trickster, so vile wicked and sinister...

Your veins are so deranged, they cringe when you play your game
You force in toxic sin you always entertain, hold your breath challenge death, see if you maintain
Push the plunger feel the thunder let's play until the end, enjoy the pain blow out your veins it's "Russian Roulette" my friend.

I am very anti-government a huge Trump supporter and ever bigger conspiracy theorist so if you know anything about those things then some of what this poem says might make sense if not I cannot clear this one up for you the secrets lie within. This poem is very subliminal and calls out a lot of things going on in the world that people are very blind to.

"Sacred Wisdom"

Were all victims of politicians
Full of lies and crooked business
Conspired suspicions lack of witness
No conviction or prison sentence
Lying women, lying with em
Yet most won't listen
So pay close attention
To the signs that glisten
The trail of lies that's given
Miles of fiction on isles of intuition
Vile resentment brings bile besetment
Filament screening leaving ferment liement
Government secrets leads to an abundant credence
Of sacrificial allegiance to the elites secretions
While the base of our pyramid collapses and weakens
Society is blinded by like minded treason
Forbade to invade the world that's beneath us
The Sky is the limit yet we gaze it to pieces
As the media deceives ya and distracting with diseases
Controlling the masses like untreated lesions
Herding the irrelevant for the Hell of it as no one believes ya
Like elephants that dance in a trance with amnesia
8 billion resilient parasites Geneva
Which is reptilian septillion cerebrum
Hidden descendants and secrets forbidden
Laid out flat before our eyes the sky has risen
Full of sin beginning to end the world has been written

Complacent towards the matrix that narrates our prison
Invasions of outrageous violent and contagious depictions
So evasive is our arrangement abrasive the missions
As we quest for a nest of alternate dimensions
A Simulation that's been vacant in a deceptive fission
Repentance is a symptom of vengeance and collision
Crimson is the witness who's own sickness of penance
Listless is his visions cause the sentence is in gimmicks
Picnics with the wicked that bring children just to visit
Do we menace all our hit list with blood of the slit wrist
Obscene as Epstein yet sects of elite's list
Stolen Souls that are sold for Diddys piece
The Devil will revel if you feed him what he needs
And "Sacred Wisdom" is hidden below our very feet!

A love poem describing why I am so hard to love and why I do or say the things I do. I wrote this for the mother of my child and hope that a lot of people both men and woman can truly relate to this one.

Sometimes

"Sometimes" I wonder what life would be like had I not met you
Would I be as wild and crazy and still treat women like I do
What if darkness surrounded me and being alone in this apartment is all I knew

"Sometimes" I think to myself that life isn't that bad
And there are worse things in the world and people far more sad
But the time spent with you I'm glad that I had, our time to interact

"Sometimes" my insecurities get the best of me, usually daily
My mind makes me think things that are way too crazy
But I put it in my own head, it ain't you it's me baby

"Sometimes" I don't know if you even believe what I say is real
I get self-conscious and scared and afraid to tell you how I feel

"Sometimes" I make all the wrong decisions
But hurting you on purpose was never my intentions
So I begged and pleaded for your forgiveness

"Sometimes" we fight for what we believe
Then in an instance we create distance as each of us leave
And were left crying on the floor, with our hearts on our sleeve

"Sometimes" I feel so guilty that I hate myself
Because it's my fault for all your pain and hell
And the love was lost from the misery felt

"Sometimes" I convince myself of the worst
For all you put up with, all that shit you don't deserve
All the lies and the times I made you cry and hurt

"Sometimes" I'm hard to read and hard to find
"Sometimes" I realize that I've been blind all this time
"Sometimes" I wish I could write deeper, more meaningful lines
"Sometimes" life is too hard to live and harder to decide
"Sometimes" I think dreaming has the most meaning when it's you who's all mine
"Sometimes" Yeah, "sometimes" I see your face when I close my eyes

Don't really have any explanation for this one I actually wrote it out of nowhere while composing this book. I guess it is another dark love poem in a sense and talks about the stain that a woman's pain can leave.

Stain of Pain

I rise and I fall and make mistakes everyday
I live and I learn and I hurt in a way
That grows and it shows in a "stain of pain"

                                    It bleeds and it leaves a terrible mark
                           That seeps through my sleeves exposing my scars
                                   So please let me be alone with my heart

If you really can't stomach me than why stay in touch
Misery loves company and bitch you visit so much
So fuck it bring your bucket paint another "stain of pain" of your love with the brush

I just wanted to write something almost out of a dark carnival something sinister and creative with a clown theme to it and this is what I came up with I guess.

"Suicide Ride"

Step inside the fucked up mind of my "Suicide Ride"
      I must advise to close your eyes cause someone might die
Gone off the road I've lost control cause I swerve when I drive
      So come with me and you will see the sick shit that I find
Some say unstable not that able to decide on what's right
      You hear the screams it's not a dream you smell the fear here tonight
So follow down this hollow path as I laugh at your life
      Along the way you see the strange & it signifies
A cynical slope with criminal hope so don't go down this slide
      Now that your lost there is a cost with this assisted suicide
And there I'll be with severed feet that wasn't tucked tight inside
      Open your eyes it's no surprise that you died on my "Suicide Ride"

This poem was written to a certain someone who kept attacking me in a very cowardly way. I don't want to say too much because this person already tried to take me to court and have a protective order put on me. Saddest excuse of a man you ever seen. Anyway I can't go into the backstory about why I wrote this but he knows!

Target

My heart is the bearer of witness
Ripped apart is the terror crimson
I'm the star of your show from start to finish

Pinching & prodding as you sift through his skin & bone
Dissecting me to pieces for reasons unknown
You put Joe through a fine tooth comb

Glorifying my horrifying moments from the past
Flashing the brand that you brandished so fast
Judging me before a court could even sentence my ass

But label he as weak is something unheard of
The Devil used to be an Angel but now that's reversed huh
You think because I fucked up I don't deserve love

Ties and connections to criminal organizations
Tried and convicted through drug accusations
Fried and committed to the prison administration

No woman in her right mind would be his wife he's too brutal
This guy's life is full of crime the red flags are unusual
He's been on 21 Alive and even all over google

I'm the reason for all your problems, yeah I caused it
Lazy and crazy, retarded and heartless
So what else you got X marks the spot I marked it
Come on take your shot aim your red dot I'm your "TARGET"

As you all point your pistols just remember one thing
Although your pointing a finger at me while you shoot and aim
you got three more pointing back at you so who's to blame

You ain't fucking perfect are lives are just different
Yeah I used and sold drugs and broke the laws as a way of livin'
I grew up rough it was tough I got fucked up and sentenced to prison
But I became a man you understand ten toes tall on the chin no snitchin'
I wasn't sheltered around fake ass bitches, hypocrites pretendin and that's the difference
So next time you want to judge me based off a biased opinion
Take a look in the mirror at your past and bad decisions
Readjust your scope just to see what's missing
So what I'm a thug, my secrets won't reach or be seen by my children
And I would never put a pistol to my head in front of them over a game system
Judge the size of our balls
Because I can admit my flaws
That's why this fuck you has been given
So as I said at the beginning and once again just listen
You shot first but remember what you said I'm vicious

And you said I won't ever be a good father to my daughter I'm heartless
But I'm a master of war so let's finish what you started
I fear no one not even death I'm dearly departed
I have no regrets I hold them dear in this compartment
I hope your aim is steady because I'm already the "TARGET".

In today's day and age the cops don't even work. They sit back while civilians that can't keep their mouth shut does all the work for them. My thoughts on snitching is that your on the same level as a rapist or sex offender if not worse. Those people take something away from a woman or child that they will never again get back or ever fully heal from mentally. Granted when we break the law and commit crimes we know we shouldn't, we understand the risk involved however let us get caught on our own. Who are you to decide to take justice in your own hands and take away our lives, take us away from our mothers, fathers, brothers, sisters, husbands, wives, our children? Usually because you got caught slipping and are in trouble yourself. Instead of accepting your fate you ruin someone else's life? That's wrongful justice. If we were to retaliate or act out on revenging a victim of another crime that would be another charge for us right? So what's the difference in what your doing? Anyway this was a poem I wrote for all the victims that have been affected by snitches myself included I have been told on by a few people and so may your souls rot in the worst parts of Hell for all eternity you low life shit balls. You know who you are the rats who got me I would include your name but you don't deserve air to breathe let alone to be featured in my book. For those who are reading this and stood solid I commend you and although you have or are currently doing time at least you can lay your head on your pillow every night with your integrity knowing you are solid.

"Teller"

Ci, Informant, Rat a bitch
Teller, Jake, police, a pinch
All Ebonic slang words for being a punk ass snitch

Picture a life where everybody you know
Solid as fuck no matter where you go

Nothing bust trust & honor amongst thieves
Loyalty at least where no one deceives

Ride or die when there was nobody else
All for one, & not all for themselves

But today that trait is so hard to find
A loyal breed it seems to be one of a kind

Fake friends pretend all the way to the end
Committing crimes then admitting their sins

To the police they sneak they can't stay true
Protecting themselves while they sell out you

Wearing wires their desire is to record what was said
Setting you up giving evidence to the feds

So all that's left is to take their life
They took yours so, it's only right!

This was just an off the topic and off the head poem I wrote and I called it The 3 Ps of Me standing for the three paragraphs that describe me best. It may not mean much to anyone else and no one may understand this one but this one is extremely dear to me.

"The 3 Ps of Me"

I put too much in the women I trust
I get way too stuck as I look for love
Only to find it was just dumb luck
And I can't quit the bitch when we kiss we fuck
But It sucks to get dumped heart on my sleeve when they leave it was only lust

My mistakes are in laid with big flakes of pain
Although the roads been paved it shows bloated shame
You provoke insane stoked the flames invoked his rage
No one knows Joes pain from the games he's played

So lay me down in a bed of sin
Crippled in my sentence of all my remanence
I shift my imminence based off critics decisions
It's given me a vison that's fueled my missions

This one is very dear to me I wrote this poem while in the throws of a very deep addiction. I was strung out and struggling with a terrible meth habit I was actually in a hotel in Ohio working on the road and in the bathroom on the floor curled up around the toilet when I wrote this and recorded it to my Tiktok if you listen to the video you can hear the pain in my voice and it will always be one of my deepest and most favorites.

The Addicts Prayer

Lonely and shallow barely visible to the eye
    I can no longer find you but mind you I try
        So I search as I lurk as I poke and I pry
        As faint traces of red regularly register inside.....

Knots and scars from all the parts I depart as painful memories
    And after years of shooting that numb rush of blood does come with ease
        But like a trigger from a gun your own thumb can kill with one squeeze....
I soon discover I have to cover my lover conceal her presence with sleeves
    I cannot resist her gifts as she shreds my soul from the toll that she leaves
        My remorse is not forced as I drop to my knees begging Jesus PLEASE!....
Whether the devil or a monkey this junkie seeks peace
    My addiction has broken me and left me to weak to speak
        This disease won't cease or release its distinct link in me....
So now I lay these veins to down to sleep>
    And if I should die from the drugs that I take
        I pray the lord don't let the next addict make the same mistakes...

This poem is very emotional and deep. I wrote this based off of real life experiences and the things I've seen through my journey and struggles in and out of addiction. The travels along the way of a man who has lost it all and became homeless and the way people see him the tears and pain through his eyes and the judgment and emotional damage that comes from outsiders as the world's cruelness comes to light.

The Backpack Man

Sometimes we can't handle the struggles and strife
We take a chance as we gamble when we play with our life
And you dance with the devil every time you roll the dice

So this is the tale of a pack and a man
A story of sorrow that's hard to understand
It's the history and misery of "The Backpack Man"

Begging just to sleep on a stranger's lawn
No money to eat and his girls long gone
He wonders through the streets with his backpack on

He hides his pride cause his minds off track
He's done strange things for that precious hit of crack
And all he has left is the pack on his back

He shivers and shakes and hasn't ate in eight days
Started asking and pan handling just for some spare change
But even the holes in his socks won't stop the rocks that he craves

His teeth are sheathed from the aliments of a fiend
Cause his lust for that rush has taken everything so it seems
Except the pack on his back that's packed with shattered dreams

You may have seen him once or twice
Sleeping at the park in the dark with no light
Scratching his head cause the bites from the lice

With dirt on his shirt and filth in his hair
There's hurt in his eyes as he sees people stare
Suicides on his mind, but would anyone care

Strapped to his back as he sat in the rain
Inflicted with addiction and consumed by pain
Stricken with this sickness as he catches a train

City to city he drifts through the land
Riddled with pity and his outstretched hand
It's the old nitty gritty "Backpack Man".

This next one is very explicit and I want to warn all the readers this may be my most controversial poem yet. I know we all have heard the stories of the Catholic Priest that molest children and how it's been happening for decades. This disgust me and pisses me off to an unexplainable point of view. I was in county jail one time and seen a huge headline on the news about this story where a bunch of them were caught doing it and fled to the Vatican where they couldn't be persecuted. What about the kids they hurt? What about them and all the suffering and pain they went through? They will never heal from that sick shit and so someone said to me "You Should Write A Poem About That" and this is what I came up with. Again this is very dark and controversial but I wanted to put awareness out there about this and although it's very graphic I still think this a very great poem and unlike anything anyone has ever written before. VIEWER DESCRETION ADVISED!!!

"The Bastard Pastor"

Wait a second Reverend this aint your normal confession
This isn't a test or a lesson it's about your obsession
With little boys under 11, I see you're sweatin, kinda stressin
Maybe second guessin you're sermon on Heaven
I brought a demon he's a mean one it's a .357 Smith & Wesson
Against your robe as I'm pressin I'm perplexin
About subjectin leaving a mess in...

This booth that you misuse for loose truth
Ten Hail Mary's is a ruse & an excuse
For the Priest at least
And the sexual abuse on the confused youth...

This man of God used to say, relax its ok
That you hope for my sake it's not too late
This is the Lords plan don't that feel great
Spread your legs and beg for forgiveness of your mistakes...

You gave me wine, told me it's fine
You said show me yours & I'll show you mine
It's all in the Bible my child trust every line
But I knew it wasn't right, you was wrong all along you lied...

Then in time, I gave up on grace
I lost my mind, I lost my faith
Such a bitter taste, I can't erase
Haunted by that fucked up look and taunted by your face...

But I do the devils work now just wait & see
You spread shame, doubt, & uncertainty
Now it's my turn to make you feel real agony...

Revenge is bitter sweet so now I'm gonna preach
As you're in the back seat of my Jeep as we creep through the streets
Hog tied & gagged, you try to scream but it's hard to breathe let alone speak
As we drive around I love the sound of your struggling as you weep...

I finally grew from the boy you once knew & abused
And the only words you ever spoke truth
Was an eye for an eye & tooth for a tooth
And now that I have all of yours loose
I think I'll put that line to good use as we conclude our little cruise...

I'll make you feel the same pain that I've felt
By taking you back to the Bible belt
Literally making that smirk on your face melt
Scraping off the layers using your carcass as a pelt...

I listen to you plead as you swing by your feet
Choking on your blood I cut out your tongue & pull out your teeth
Preach it Preacher come on PREACH!!!

Behold the words from the days of old
Your punishment tonight will be 7 fold
To messy to be told these unthinkable actions are bold
Cause you turned my innocent heart stone cold...

Enjoying the sounds of you wail as I pierce your palms with the nail
Dripping a red mascaraed of a bloody trail
This is my Picasso you look so helpless and frail...

Jesus died for our sins he didn't pretend or lie
He looked towards the sky asking Father why
.... So did I
You Bastard Pastor it's your time to lose your life
I start at your thighs as I skin you alive...

Down to the bone as I deliver you home
To the devil in Hell so you can be molested on his throne...

This poem was just a crazy concept I came up with one day. I just thought about how I could write a poem that depicts being buried alive. Something short and simple but equally creative.

The Box Is Locked

As you open your eyes you can't see a thing
You're air is scarce and it's hard to breathe
You cry for help as you bellow and scream
But "The Box is Locked" as your ears only ring

    With only inches to move around
    You wiggle and squirm, cry and shout
    Feeling the wood that closely surrounds
    Yet "The Box is Locked" with you in the ground

        You cry out to God as you beg and pray
        Clawing the top till your nails rip away
        Numb to the blood and dumb to the pain
        And "The Box is Locked" but you're here to stay

Time is running out if you could just sit up
You can tell from the thuds that there's earth above
But ashes to ashes and dust to dust
As "The Box is Locked" you're stuck you're fucked just shit out of luck

    Reality begins to set in as your head spins nervously
    You were buried alive by someone you knew personally
    And there's no way out that's a for sure certainty
    You're trapped inside this box for all eternity...

I wrote this while going through a really tough breakup and I was really tore up mentally and emotionally at the time I was put through Hell by this woman and so I do what I do best I put that bitch in a poem. Hurt me and I'll make you famous.

The Break Up

They lie they cheat
Betrayal Deceit
Replay Repeat
Accepting Defeat
Broken and Hopeless to the point you can't breathe

I've known all along
The hatred's so strong
I can't stay calm
Goodbye, so long
I want to die but suicide is justified all wrong

The doctors suggest
I get some rest
Forget the past try not to stress
Get on with my life move onto the next
I just can't seem to breath with this deep wheeze in my chest

Shattered like glass
It happened so fast
The conclusions are rash
But the confusion won't pass
Drive to a different dimension of a demented relapse

I write a lot of evil sounding poems at times and a lot of people say that I am being evil and wicked myself. But that's NEVER the case I actually am Baptized and really believe in God and Jesus as my lord and savior I pray all the time and I admit I am far from a devout Christian by the book man who has it all figured out because I am far from where I should be but I do believe and try hard within my faith. I write things like this for a different reason. One being that I like the creativity I can come up with and two because there is always an underlying message or reason behind why I write my dark stuff like this one. I knew a guy who kept denouncing God and acting crazy he blasphemed a lot and practiced Witchcraft so I wrote this as a sort of message as to how he felt and where he was going in life and especially in his afterlife. My purpose was maybe he would read something that he liked or related to that he found entertaining and amusing but with an alternative ending as to what his fate surely would be. In essence I wanted to show him how foolish he was and hopefully scare him in the end. And I just happened to write and poem out of it.

The Devil's Love Letter

My minds a go and set to spin
My play pen is Satan's den
The demons within are drenched in sin
They play pretend and always win
Evil pen pals with no pen
Vile smiles with a wicked grin

                      Dark and leery heart is eerie
                      Black and cold my soul is dreary
                      Screams but it seems no one's near me
Except Lucifer and the rumor is only he can hear me

                      Verily verily, quite contrary
                      I hear voices very scary
                      Drifting down the sound is weary
                      Gripping claws that maw and tear me
                      It hurts and burns, in turns they share me

            Demonic monsters lob and toss
            This black veil and broken cross
            The devil fell without a loss
            Cause I'm in hell and he's the boss

Hands down this is my all-time most favorite poem and will always be my number one. It's also the very first one I ever recorded on my Tiktok so in reality this is what I owe all my success to. This is what got me famous and notoriety on social media. I wanted to describe a love story that was deeper than any other love tale and so as it begins you are tricked into thinking it is really about a love story about a woman the ending has a remarkable but chilling twist.

The Evil Needle

I love my bitch but she's psychotic
Our relationship is long & strong but all wrong & toxic
Yet our sex is the best she's so erotic
My girl is different unique & exotic
But she's this wicked sickness that gets so intense it's chronic
Her strain is hard on my heart it's part chaotic
And when I don't have my lover I shudder under the covers as I shake and vomit

Her looks are deadly fatal & brutal
She's my dose my daily my usual
Yeah my baby maybe crucial
She always saves me she gave me renewal
She's so tasty crazy but useful
Her beauty makes my eyes go wide as my pupils quadruple

She pushed away all my family & all my friends
I gambled my life when I let her win
I surrendered too her sin & the relentless trend
Pleasure came & went just as the happiness did
She became the reason my misery didn't end
So I fake this face as I make it pretend

But she just won't leave she never stays away
She always comes back so we can play
Polluting my mind till it's cloudy with rain
Consuming my heart, my lungs, and my brain

And arguing with her only leaves me drained
How you conceal but won't heal her scars I crave
So I wear these sleeves to deceive what we all call pain

I'm weak with her disease defeated and feeble
Misery loves company and that's all that we equal
This girl is a curse she's my church and the steeple
I fell for her hurt the lies and the people
And this is my love story of **"THE EVIL NEEDLE"**

I didn't know where I was going with this one I just wanted to write something about life being a game and how there's always other players and someone trying to take you out or beat you.

The Games Over

It's the only thing on my mind, another crime another day
I get so high, I go blind, but it don't make the hatred go away
This world is a challenge, and it's all in how you play

Ridicule is fuel and you make do with what your dealt
But it's my shuffle, so I'm dealing out all that I felt

I use the abuse cause love turns sour
I manipulate with hate hour by hour, that's how you win, by having power

Whether multiplayer or a single man conquest, you want the victory you want to be best
We all want that title or ribbon on our chest
Like an inner beast that won't let us rest
An impossible riddle the ultimate test
Showing up to battle with an S on your bulletproof vest

A pawn within reason
Gone is the season
Wrong missin pieces
Long driven treason

We fight for first place
A steady run of race
Fun is the pace
No gun just mace

You surrender you lose
Remember we choose
So enter the room
The Games Over but it's your move.

Another song I wrote about a man just drifting by through life and wondering on and on with no purpose or belonging.

"The Lonely Man"

Verse 1-   Lonely as the cloud that's slowly
Floating somewhere round here going
Into the sky, as my mind passes me by
I wonder why?
I start to cry

Verse 2-   Swallow his own innocence.
He's living in this sinful bliss
His hollowed emptiness begins
He's falling in this endless pit
He wonders why?
He starts to cry

Chorus-   He's been on his own
For oh so long
So, on and on it goes
And on and on it goes

Verse 3-   Filtering the ashes, of this shattering masochist
He wonders why?
He starts to cry

Chorus-   He's been on his own
For oh so long and,
On and on it goes
On and on it goes
On and on and on it goes

This one is really cool because its written in actual letter form, yet a poetic story that rhymes and has a pretty. Sad meaning. I wrote from a father to his Son from Prison.

The Next Prison Letters

My son, it's good to hear from you, sorry it's been a few
Gotta life of your own the world has plenty to do
Growin every day and your about to be twelve too...
I write you from my cell, it's my home it's my Hell
Not your fault though, I did this to myself
It's still hard for me to tell, you that I'm sorry I failed
But I pray for you every day, that life suits you real well...
So many nights alone, I've sat and cried
Thoughts of suicide resonate deep inside
But then I close my eyes and picture you by my side...
Wish I could pick you up after school, swim with you in the pool
Teach you to work on cars, mow the yard or play with tools
But I made too many mistakes, your pops is a fool...
I blame myself for everything you never had
Growin up without your Dad, makes me so sad, it just hurts so bad
I wish I could go back, and put our lives on track...
I wish I could change the past, life is beautiful Son so make it last
Because just as quickly as it comes, it goes just as fast...
But I know you're gonna be a better man than me
I wish I could see you turn sixteen, just live your life boy please be free...
You asked what it was like in here, it's simple, it's brutal
Last week a guy died just over a noodle, so I stick to myself, I read, write, and doodle...
It gets hard on the yard knowin you ain't comin home
Sometimes I feel so alone, collect calls on broken phones
This is the last life I'll ever know...

It will break the strongest of men, knowin that never again can you hold your kid

What more is there to say when the state puts you away

Locked up is more than just a show when you're really livin the extended stay...

I love you Son, now and forever, you make my days better

So until we meet again in the next prison letter.

This next one is just something I came up with from an idea that someone had sparked inside of my mind. I was facilitating a class in a program inside of prison and I had said something one day during one of my lessons and a guy come up to me after class and said you could really use your pain as something powerful so that sparked the idea for this poem.

The Power of Pain

I had to come up on my own
Livin in broken homes, goodwill clothes
And shoes too small they hurt my toes
Accounts begin and end in zeros
With no assets to be froze
No one knows the roads I've walked alone
All my paths were over grown
Although it came slow
All that shit I let go
A rose will find a way it always grows
So through the mud I arose
It still hurts but I'll never show
You can still see the scars if you look close

I found me without the need
Of my parents I'm just off their offspring
Maybe a waste of good seed
So I pour my heart out on these sheets
And use my blood for the ink
I gave up on my defeat
And said fuck being beat
Because I'm unique
There's a cryptic mystique when I speak
Sometimes it's clean and neat even sweet
Then I write some off the wall shit that's mean and obscene
But this is me my poetry's deep
It grabs you and has you on the edge of your seat

Pulling you to your feet, leaving you weak
It's like doin meth and tryin to go to sleep

Do you think there's a way or something to say
To erase the misplaced hate that was made
Just to create this disarray on my face
Feeling like such a waste a disgrace
But I embrace this world it's a cold place
That's why I been writing since I was eight
To escape to you it may seem plain
But to those that can relate never under estimate
<u>The Power of Pain</u>

So look inside, back behind
These brown eyes and try to decide
Is it pain or pride that I use to drive
It's been a rough and tough ride
Once or twice, considered suicide
It's hard to live but easy to die
Instead I decided to write my life
Through these lines one at a time

So when I die I don't want fortune or fame
I don't want to win any type of game
Just that people remember the Easterday name
And hopefully one day someone can relate
Through <u>The Power of Pain</u>

I was at a place called RDC (Regional Diagnostic Center) it's the place you go to before prison to be classified and placed determining your level what prison you're going to go to. Let me tell you in my opinion it is the absolute worst part of prison. Lockdown 23 hours a day to big or to small raggedy jumpsuits, used yellow piss stained boxers and socks the toilets only flush twice every hour so if you or your Bunkie have to shit you can't courtesy flush. It is your first taste of prison food before you get to a real yard. You get a shower every 3 days for 5 minutes and it's the most ice cold freezing shower you have ever taken in your life. The mats you sleep on are covered in every bodily fluid that can come from the human body and stains that cannot be explained. The cells are so tiny that you can lay in your bunk and touch every part of the cell from reaching you're arms out. No phone calls, no visits, and you are only allowed out to watch movies once a day but it is VHS movies. Twister, Titanic, Meet The Browns, Pretty Woman, they even played Broke Back Mountain one time for a bunch of harden criminal men in prison (yeah not a very entertaining movie considering the script and the environment. Needless to say this place is Hell and I hate it. I have had the pleasure of being accommodated in the luxury of this facility on several occasions and it gets shittier every time. The worst part is what it does to your mentality and your spirit so when I wrote this poem this was where I was in my cell going crazy and wanting to write my girl at the time.

These Bars

Countless nights under these stars
Holding onto hope as I grope "These Bars"

Broken pieces of me shatter to shards
And only you can mend me back inside "These Bars"

Pictures and messages and the phone calls are hard
Only because I can't touch you inside "These Bars"

Trapped inside they caged my heart
But nothing can keep us apart, not even "These Bars"

I wanted to write a really personal poem that talks about everything that I have witnessed and lived throughout my life. The things that I don't agree with or the sorrows and struggles that I have seen firsthand. Actual friends that committed actual crimes and are actually still in prison. I'm sorry for the mistakes I have made and the things my close dudes have done but they still are my guys and I wanted to include them in this poem. Actual events that have happened in my life. I don't condone my past and I'm and not proud of the life and choices I have made but I can't take them back and I do not regret who I was. It's made me who I am today. I still do not and WILL never support or condone snitching or the cases of sex offenders of any sort and the content in this next poem is my feelings on that. It gets a little vulgar a I say some pretty harsh things but this poem was written while I was in prison and I wanted to show case the man behind the book so this is very personal but an exact timeline and clip of my life through my eyes and what it was like walking in my shoes.

This Is My Life

This world is so cold & out of control
And I admit my flaws & that I've come close
To giving up & letting go
I've been backed against the ropes
Banged & slanged dope, overdosed
Been on top, flopped fallen so below, been broke
Choked on smoke to the point I almost croaked
Betrayed by bros & self-righteous hoes
Friends that were pretend turned out to be my foes
Brought em to my home when they had nowhere to go
Broke bread but they fed on whole loaves
Picked from my wardrobe, they wore my own clothes
But I suppose we all know, peoples intentions eventually shows
I've loved & been hurt both more than most
Had someone step on every one of my toes
Been forced into church but couldn't cope
Locked up so much I've lost all hope
Seen some foul things done some even gross
So I decided to put it in a poem and this is how it goes....

If you don't believe then you need to see
Please feel free to read you shall receive
This wisdom that bleeds from me
And the things that I've seen are written on these sheets

Since I was young I was raised never to tell
But when it comes to drugs I felt compelled

To display it all upon a shelf
But the only limelight is on myself
I'd never judge or roll or anyone else
I fell victim to the spell, getting high was my Hell
I been doing this shit ever since I was 12

As we proceed there's no need to be alarmed
Indeed I'm sure your charmed
I was dealt a life that was hard
But I stayed & played all my cards
It led me to prison yards, pills then shards
Call it self-inflicting harm
But I don't cut, it's a needle I put in my arm

But before it could put me in a hearse, laid to rest in the dirt
All those around me devastated & hurt
I tried to reimburse my subscription at the church
But they viewed my prescriptions as a curse
That made my addiction worse
They treated me like a junkie, that little twerp
Said fuck me those judgmental fuckin jerks
Fire and fire don't mix were both gonna burn
Can't afford rehab I'm not insured
The payments are outrageous it's so absurd
Control I never had guess I'll never be cured
Aint got nothin left so come on death it's my turn

So I need not mention I have a problem with religion
I got cruel intentions, and my own ambitions

Neurons can't be fixed, but I'm too quick to be tricked by this suspicious shit
I don't need a witness just to quit the gimmicks

And I'm in disgust, because the system is so corrupt
The judge don't want to budge so he must hold a grudge
Against us thugs who use drugs
He wants to fuss at us for whatever it was
A drug addict does like catchin a buzz
Then were supposed to trust that his rulings fair & just

That he made the right decision for the petty crimes I was committin
I deserve to be sentenced to prison
Snitches pointin fingers as the jury just listens

Yet when it comes to a child molester
He'll be set free before the start of next school semester
His worst punishment is that he has to register
They should sentence torture to a predator
Like a valve building pressure
Nothing makes me fester quite like a chester
Prowling the parks after dark looking for their next treasure

And please explain this how a low life bitch with 6 kids
Sells her food stamps & sucks 10 dicks just to get a quick fix
It aint cool cause when it comes to school those kids always miss
When they do go they smell like shit and piss
And have bed bug bites that that look like zits
Bruises on their arms, starved, black eyes & fat lips
But will respond to a call from a nosy neighbor about some nonsense

How can CPS allow this shit it don't make sense

So where's the justice at?
Do we get fucked with a gavel or a baseball bat
Don't answer that, in fact
The legal system is all a trap
And if you can show me fair I'll tip my hat

Cause I know some killers that are lifelong friends
Like Mike, Ol Nike, Justin, and Ryan Richison
Call em side kicks in a sense
It's sad their doing such long or life bits
In their case they couldn't acquit
Cause the glove did fit
Fuck OJ his money got him out of that shit
It's a shame in this game when you gotta sit
On trial sometimes for a crime you legit didn't commit
But some of my dudes are really guilty of what they did
And it did stick and all the hurt they caused the innocent
Or facing a dope case cause a bitch snitched
When they say you did it you'll feel so sick
The case gets intense because it's your life in defense
And if you lose you'll die behind a fence
All this may seem senseless but here's my consensus
If you snitch you need to die in a ditch and then get
Covered in lye & piss as you lie in shit & fry in the abyss
And hopefully while in the fiery pit it never ends and you can't quit
And your forced to suck 66 dicks till your sick
Then do it again you rat ass bitch

Were born to live yet born to die
Every day spent racing towards your demise
So while were alive, why do some people spend their whole lives
Spitting venom & lies it's unwise, victims on the rise
Shit balls who compromise then deny
Don't be surprised
Because integrity today is regularly despised
But this is what I see <u>This Is My Life</u>.....

"This Lonely Road" is very special to me and means a lot I wrote this while I was in SEG in prison it will always be one of my favorite poems of mine and really expresses a mental state of my mind that I was trapped in for a long time.

This Lonely Road

Lost in the shadows I'm scared and stuck
Can't find my way cause I'm drunk as fuck

Stare into my eyes and describe what you see
A mind full of hate and a heart full of need

All you hear is the caw of the crow
He's black as me on "THIS LONELY ROAD"

Too afraid that I can't have fun
I'm so paranoid that I sleep with a gun

I fall to my knees as I scream at death
I cheat him all the time but he never rests

Waves of pain each day is all I know
And tomorrow's full of sorrow on "THIS LONELY ROAD"

Church don't work cause I don't believe
That there is even a God it's just odd to me

I can't find happiness even in myself
I've looked for joy in the ways of wealth

Surrounded by trees that will never grow
Just like my dreams on "THIS LONELY ROAD"

Broken by pain as I stay in the dark
Blood on my sleeve there's a stain from my heart

Divided as I revel alone in my cell
Fighting with the devil as we dance here in hell

Deep inside I just feel so alone
Everyone's gone on "THIS LONELY ROAD"

Hung up on a girl and the hurt wont erase
I'm trapped in a world as I search for my place

A labored sigh every time I try to breathe
So it should be my choice if I decide to leave

Friends begin but always end as foes
Nothing never lasts but the tracks of "THIS LONELY ROAD"

Love is a mirage and it don't exist
I'll paint the page with the blood from my wrist

Along the way you'll notice the hurt
Cause there's nothing to say when the bridge is burnt

Running from my past but I'm moving slow
I'm trapped on the path of "THIS LONELY ROAD"

My silhouettes the only friend in sight

And he's only around in the dead of night

My fear of rejection is a deeming excuse
But it's a type of infection I'm destined to use

Depressions a lesson I'm guessing so prone
But it's a question of reflection on "THIS LONELY ROAD"

I cut myself as a release of pain
And I smile sometimes just to cut through the rain

Questing for the light but I end up going blind
I'm drowning in my sick cause its twisted in my mind

So walk with me through the cold unknown
The journey won't stop on "THIS LONELY ROAD"

This was just an odd poem that I wanted to describe my mental health at the time and what it's like to want to give up because you become so tired of dealing with everything in life and depression consumes you

"TIRED"

I'm so TIRED but not in the literal sense
      This gets way more intense!!!
It's more or less a mental stress
      That won't let you rest and never quits!!!
Buried alive as I lie on my side in the coffin
      Trying to survive before I die but I can't quit coughin
I'm gawkin at the awkward stability that I'm visually stalkin
      TIRED from all the voices that won't stop talkin
TIRED from my shadow that won't stop walkin
      Clinging to swinging like I'm always golfin
TIRED of my vices that are reachin & clawin
      Only to end up flawlessly fallin
There I go again against the wind & stallin
      Wired with disease, tIRED with fatigue
In a bind and dire need
      For my mind to be at ease
Cause this sick in me don't ever sleep
      It just won't cease or bring me peace
It's so hard to breathe
      When it's a hunger you can't feed
I'm so TIRED of everyone under the sun that wants to see me fail
I'm so TIRED of living life on the run with no avail
I'm so TIRED of being weak and frail
This decree is in me to speak while on my knees & pale
I'm TIRED of trying to describe the right type of beginning to my never ending tale

IM JUST SO TIRED......

Another Mom poem. I wrote this just as an appreciation to my Mother and all that she has done far from one of my best but I still wanted to include it in my book.

To My Mama

You've always been there with a quickness
Through my drama, and through my sickness
But my Mama never kept me waiting long

So I say this without gimmicks
Mom I know it's been a minute
But I want to say I'm sorry for all my wrongs

I put you through so much shit
But you're the only Mother that I get
I pray you'll forgive me, even for half of it

The best of me is all you
And the rest of me is too
I'm thankful for all that you do
The greatest parent that I ever knew

Far back as I can remember, and way back when
Mama you've always been my best friend
So let me say before this poem is done
You'll always be my number one
And I'm blessed to be, your first son
I love you Mom, ever since our story begun

This next one was really hard to write. My Dad although not my real Father he was the only one I've ever known for reasons un-known to me the first time he ever met me this man says to me, "I don't know what it is about you but you're my Son from here on out" as he looked me up and down. I laughed it off thinking it was just a joke but I had no idea the seriousness of that man's words and the depth of love that he would give me for the rest of his life. He really loved me like his own Son and he became my Dad. I don't speak on my situation about my Father very often because it's a very touchy subject. But I loved this man with all that I was and he became sick with cancer and I knew that I didn't have long. I couldn't bring myself to write this poem for him even though he asked me after he was diagnosed. But finally he got really bad and was sent home to die. I couldn't wait any longer I knew time was very limited so I broke down and with every word and hours staring at the blank pages I cried and wrote this very hard poem. It was so hard to write let alone read. It was a Friday I took it over to let him hear it and he passed away that next Saturday morning it was world ending for so many but I'm just thankful I finished it before he died. Somehow I was able to read it at his funeral. I miss him more than I could ever begin to describe and love him with all that I am I am so thankful for my pops so this was for him.... I love you Dad

To My Pops (David Hartman)

It's presumed that we're scolded to teach us wrong from right
So that we become groomed and molded through the time line of life

Yearning for guidance and reasons to stay in compliance
It takes a man to raise a man that type of role model is priceless

I will forever argue that blood is thicker than water
Because most my family I actually seem to bother
Even without relation you showed no hesitation to become my father

So from the ashes I climb
Exact and intact in fact I rise
Blessed because I have the best father of all time

You loved me abundantly and so unconditionally
It was more than enough as it was done unintentionally
No matter my drama, decisions, or mistakes
You were there for me Poppa relentless in your grace
And since day one you always gave your Son a place to stay

I cherish our memories although not enough
The past didn't last as it seemed so rushed
My heart will once again break from the ache without your Fatherly love
But I'll see you again Dad till then rest easy because you've done enough

The goodbyes in our eyes are flooded with tears and surprise
It's the worst kinda hurt when someone close to you dies
As the people who remain somehow refrain from their lives

The words that I write in these lines with each verse
It's hard on my heart I can't express the hurt
I love you Pops even after your time stops here on earth
I hope Heaven has Harleys because the sky is yours

R.I.P. Dad I miss you so much...

Short and cute love poem that's cheesy but sweet.

"Together We Stand"

Everything about you is heavenly
And un-questionably you and me were destined to be

You're more precious than diamonds, gems, or gold
And I hope to prosper with you long after were old

A saving grace that made me change my ways
I love you now and forever till my last days

I found solace through our path of time
In a trance I woke to find you by my side

Amazed at your beauty and your gorgeous gaze
The look of an Angel with a smile on your face

Here we are hand in hand
Against the world "Together We Stand"

I was just snapping one day and writing and seeing how long I could keep the same rhyme going and how long and sensible I could make the poem. I think it was pretty creative. I've said it before but EMINEM, CHECK ME OUT DOG!

Tongue Twister

While you're bumpin' your gums and twirlin' your thumbs

Huffin' and puffin' I might be on to something other than not givin' a fuck about nothin' I'm a hillbilly thug who's tough and rugged and close to combustion or an obscure abduction and I'm sure your pay grades way above it so if you don't mind take a hike you dike go find a bucket and fuck it and be so kind as to take a dive on my dick and suck it there's no need to pass judgement but you're bad at bluffin' I know it's sad and disgustin' just because it's hard for me to function' without the mass consumption of a bunch of drugs til I get high as fuck and numb and dumb from all the unjust corruption that comes with the fun of lust and seduction I know there's no trust from sluts that are suckin' or a junky husband a ruckus of stubborn that's stuck n stutterin' from shootin' up just pickin' and pluckin' but high just because I'm sufferin' from a robust rush of a tussionex brunched & bunched with a bunch of robitussin so stop the fuckin' fussin' and take your normal life and shove it cause this crazy life is mine and I fuckin' love it.

DISCLAIMER!!! So this next poem is going to shock and disgust most readers. It's called Twisted Thoughts. Now I like to write a lot of crazy off the wall material. Sometimes I go as far as I can push it and say things that are so despicable and crazy that it may make most readers or listeners cancel me. However when I write this absurd literature I go for the AW factor I want total shock and just people left with jaw dropping confusion and mind fuckery. None of it is factual or true none of it is glorifying or portraying anything I actually think about. I simply try to just come up with the absolute most dysfunctional illustrations I could ever create. So here is it is (NO JUDGMENT IM ONLY BEING CREATIVE)

"Twisted Thoughts"

Listen you don't want to miss this...
I'm going to tell you a tale about a man that's relentless
No forgiveness for his sins he tends to commit
No amount of men can mend or bend this quick son of a bitch
He's TWISTED, demented and listless a psycho that needs to be committed
I had a license to dissect and infect but they've been suspended
Speaking in third person again that's just it I can't quit I'm senseless
With all these visions of prison mixin with a hint of discontent it's stupendous
The way I express this sick shit so vivid I'm like a wicked ventriloquist

I didn't choose this, but don't confuse this, because I do put good use to this
And It's the reason for all the excuses and why that is that I'm so secluded
For the loose screws I produce I'm a nuisance and my ego is covered in bruises
Born to lose, tattooed and illusive but screw it I'm fluent
A little paranoid and that's translucent but who are you to deduce
Who can see through it stupid at least I keep my demons congruent
And so what if I choose to use my two new blue shoes as a 13 loop Noose
Who else would do it and who else yells for help while there poopin

I stay upset, cause I don't know what the voices in my head said and due to the psych meds I still see the tattered threads from my wife's dress that I shred

There was so much blood I was covered in red

She started to bloat way worse than when we wed

I slit her throat and watched as she bled then made her choke as I fucked her neck

While I did some coke on the edge of the bed

As I took pics with the bitch long after she was dead

Waiting on the feds to digest this horrible mess

And I quote "The Prisoner Confessed To This Sinister Dread"

There's no need for leads we have the prisoner under arrest

My mind and heart turn over but there's no spark, but I still will quilt in the dark

As I ride stilts built by Tony Stark, I tend to laugh when I fart

Like a retard shark swimming around Noah's Ark

Jumping out of the water just to bark at the hard aardvark

Driving his go kart that's falling apart while doing shards as he sharts

And breaks hearts cause valentines cards are body parts wrapped as mars bars

I crush up a few Flintstones like there percs in the pew of a church

Snortin the shit till my nose hurts

Trying to peek up a sleek petit tea cup butt of a nun and feel her up

I'm berserk and my dick won't work so show me yours and let's take turns

They say you get what you deserve I guess I'm gonna burn from all my absurd nerve

But I just want a permed nerd that squirts when she flirts and has a bush like a fern

I'm such a charming motherfucker but it's a wonder
I aint been caught under the covers by some dumb cunts crazy ex-lover
Or the sluts older brother I'm unstable and there's none other
I'm seeing sounds and hearing color and I still breast feed on my unwilling Mother
Cat scans shows a man that wears a rubber on his plunger
And lived in a hummer with no bumper all last summer
What's right with this guy well that's a whole lot tougher to discover
So onto the next verse unless you want to continue to suffer

I can paint a darker picture kids killed quicker
Strung and hung by their own suspenders
Thicker whicker zipper rippers
Cut off their eyelids with toe nail clippers then feed em through a wood chipper
Like a brand new baby in a half used blender
Beat their pets to death with Grandmas slippers
Lock up Free Willy then snip off his flippers
I'm a demented sick trickster that's sinister
Kidnap my parents and hold them prisoner
And make em watch as I rape my dead little Sister

So look inside my fried mind and you'll find me
Back behind the blind eyes of someone evil as can be
A grotesque mess, possessed and obsessed is he
Incest but I'm blessed because my cousins legally 13
These are my "Twisted Thoughts" for the day you won't believe what I see......

This is a very intricate poem that I did about a dark personality with a man who suffers from mental disorders and that's very disconnected with himself and the world around him but a little crazy. I think the rhyming patterns are very compatible and flow together nicely. EMINEM HIRE ME!!!

"Unstable"

So much distance missin' from reality losin' my own shit
Just the remanence of a sociopath that's in and out of it
Disassociation rendered in a helpless state of dement
Nothing seems to register even as I vent
What's the point of livin' if I'm dyin' with these sins I tend to commit
Stricken by this sickness to wicked to repent

Slowly hopin' my emotions will get the best of me
In a lonely coma thats eroded me mentally
Losin' focus as I'm choking on sanity
Eyes are swollen cause I'm goin' on no sleep

Evil lurks like a hearse that's been cursed upon my grave
So write a verse make it hurt on my headstone let it say
I was observed and berserk shovel the dirt away
I yearn just to burn put me in my place
Guess I'll learn cause it's my turn my souls the one at stake

A little unhinged and not that able
To sit with the normal around the table
Voices in my head like horses in the stable
Being led astray like a puppet with its cables
I talk back to my voices because I'm 'Unstable'

This poem was written as an inner self. It is me basically describing the captions of my life and feelings my emotions and journey. The pain I have felt mixed with addiction, depression, neglect, abandonment, all my insecurities and the frail man that's left alone in the shadows.

Vacant Says the Sign

Vacant says the sign
      Alone in my own mind

Nowhere left to run
      Loaded as the gun

Tomorrow's all that's real
      And sorrow's all I feel

Faded from the hurt
      And hated like a curse

The only thing that's left
      Is the faint clouds of my breath

That disappear into the sky
      Joined by tears with shame I cry

Vacant says the sign
      Yet sheltered is my pride

Pain is what remains
      It courses through my veins

So low the grounds above me
      Seems to me no one loved me

I can't take much more
> Made bitter to the core

Rusted as a can
> And empty stands the man

Lonely is all I find
> *Vacant Says The Sign*

This was just some crazy sadistic one I wrote to try and bring some insight into the life of an addict and what he sees through his addiction and only someone who's been there can relate to these metaphors and examples that I used. This was a very low and dark place for me and I pray for anyone who ever has had to live this life. AND BY NO MEANS when I write things like this am I glorifying these behaviors it's just my struggles with these terrible battles.

Veinfull

Filling the spoon at noon with this debris
10 units of water and soon it dissolves instantly
It begins as a shard started crystally
Don't use a cotton there's just no need
I suck up the solution the pollution it's slow to see
Like a lotus below us that pokes us with his feet
He's focused as the needle accepts it's eager treat
with a quick flip the of the rig 2 watch with glee
The bubble switch from end to end jubilee
I push the tip into my skin the pain is comforting as it beautifully stings
I know that seconds from now I'll be numbingly buzzingly like a bee
Tingling and fluttery maybe possibly on the verge of an OD
Ahh there it is it's finally complete
As a mushroom cloud of blood erupts violently
Mixing and swirling as it combines inside the tube combiningly
This poison I crave inside of me
Eyes wide and dilated like they're meant to be supposedly
I Jam the plunger down excitedly
And plunge almost as if its pushing me
And as the mix hits I almost do the splits and twists and get sick from it's toxicity
Entering me so fast and roughly
I feel my heart rate race increasingly
Gasping and breathing rapidly and so suddenly it's so hard to see
I can feel my hair extend and split seemingly

looks like a survived a ride down Tweaker Street geekingly
Fried and spun as my tongue is numb it's so hard for me to speak
Sleeplessly deprived already on day three
Shadow people swing freely from the trees
Time for another shot I must increase the need
To support my destructiveness enabling my disease
Although the range full and inlaid strange and fully deranged yet painful is thee
You can be keep your Ovaltine I'll take another vein full please

This was just a creative poem I did to paint this picture of what someone who suffers from mental health goes through and all the insecurities they may feel within themselves. How they hear voices and never feel good enough or like they are not ok.

If you or anyone you know are suffering with mental health or feeling suicidal please know that you are not alone. And I know you have heard that a lot and its cliché but so many people truly suffer and there are so many people who are afraid to speak up and ask for help for fear of rejection or judgment, shame or embarrassment please know that I have suffered from so much torment and mental health myself and if there is one goal I hope to accomplish with my poetry it's to reach even just one person and save someone from these feelings of never being good enough or like something is wrong with them that can't be fixed. We all suffer from something, none of us are perfect but there are still wonderful people of there that care. I care about you and If you need to talk to someone feel free to reach out to me on any of my social media or website.

"Voices"

"Voices" they talk & whisper
      They fade away like a stray drifter

      In my ears they ring &
In my dreams the scream

"Voices" they echo & shout
      These seeds they sprout

      Growing and blowing
            As a windless sound

"Voices" haunting & exotic
      Taunting & demonic

      This noise toys with my mental stability
            As it rapes & destroys vast and vividly

"Voices" misleading & breathing
      As my conscience is speaking & constantly depleting

Blind from its disguise
      It's silently defeating

"Voices" for days in waves they stay
      Clouding my mind & gouging my brain

I'm battling time &
    I'm fighting this pain

"Voices" tear inside of me
    Everywhere I go

    Taking what they please
        & leaving me alone

VOICESVOICESVOICESVOICESVOICESvoices

I have a habit of taking popular sayings or quotes and making them into my own poems. This one included. I related it to my addiction when in recovery you often hear that the definition of insanity is doing the same thing over and over again expecting deferent results which is true. However I twisted mine around my drug addiction.

What Is Insane?

So What is Insane?
> Is it the plain Jane façade we maintain full of disarray, pain and distain
> Why do we live this way and play so much in the dope game
> As our lives are led astray, having to look into the mirror just for someone to blame
> Well I must say my motives are critically acclaimed and wickedly the same
> So vividly these dreams came, pure serenity and instantly went down the drain

So What is Insane?
> Doing the same thing over and over each day
> While you watch those who chose to love you walk away
> Putting a needle in your arm seems to be okay
> That we can somehow hide our problems deep down in our veins
> Just pretend to depend on the pills, the meth, heroin or cocaine
> As we spent our last cent and every dollar we've ever made
> Sold our shit or gave it away in a dope fiend trade
> Pay attention and listen as once again I say

So What is Insane?
> That we would go to the ends of the earth just to obtain
> One more hit just a pinch for the brain
> Say fuck your kids for a quick fix just a little bit of a head change

Been gone so long that they forgot your name
Three of your friends found dead in some drug-related way
Everyone else is for themselves and have nothing to say
Except askin' you for shit so y'all can get straight
Drown out the sorrows let your heart rate fade
While your friends in their graves being lowered into their final resting place
They don't care about you only that you continue to make mistakes
Misery loves company they're each other's soul mate

If you have ever felt something electric or magnetic right when you meet someone it could have been love at first sight or just a lustful attraction but either way you felt emotions and feelings that you hold onto. This was my meaning behind this poem.

"When I Saw You"

"When I saw you"
You looked so cute, a few tattoos
I knew it was you who I wanted by my side
Sparks flew, our connection grew, it was such a lovely surprise

"When I saw you"
I fell in love that first time we locked eyes
Hottest country girl in the world I can't deny
Yet you were deep in the streets, always down to ride
Johnny & June mixed with Bonnie and Clyde

"When I saw you"
It felt like I had known you my whole life
Those thick hips and luscious lips, damn you look fine
But I had to say goodbye and go do some time

"When I saw you"
My life was hell, I was lost and empty and so unwell
Cursed by my demons under my own spell
So at the time there was no way I could tell
You that I loved you and how I felt
But "When I saw you" I'd always melt

"When I saw you"
Our timing was always wrong
So I had to wait and be strong
And pray to God you wouldn't move on

Cause I had to have you no matter how long
I was gonna take a chance we were meant to be all along

"When I saw you"
Our lives was a mess, neither of us could pass a piss test
There was still so much I had to confess
From my past and all the shit I regret
So it was hard to pretend I wasn't upset
With my life at the times, but I did my best
You're so unique and different from all the rest
I would dream of holding you, your head on my chest

"When I saw you"
It was at my all-time low. Everything lost and nothin to show
Faking happiness just so no one knows, broken inside as the misery grows
Losing hope, consumed by dope, I couldn't cope and was just ready to explode
And "When I saw you" you knew I was close to giving up and just letting go

"When I saw you"
I was beatin down, defeated, un-needed no one else around
In search of something safe and sound
I was drowning in mud already 6 feet deep in the ground
But someone saved me and pulled me out, I looked up and it was you I found

"When I saw you"

It was in my dreams, you and me, on the scene a life together a successful team

Pure happiness a beautiful thing, I want for nothing cause you're all I need

You give me faith and reason to believe, I love you baby so please don't leave

"When I saw you"

It was after I closed my eyes last night, I wrapped my arms around you, kissed you, and held you tight

Nothing in this world ever felt so right

"When I saw you"

It was when I woke up, I opened my eyes to your picture hung above, imagining your touch, kiss and hugs

You're my new addiction I can't get enough, thank you for saving me my little dove

"When I saw you" I knew it was true love

Just a short quirky love poem I came up with that shows my appreciation for a strong woman and what she means to me. Her troubled past her pain and hurt and all the things she has overcome. Still able to smile through the misery and push through the tough times.

"When She Smiles"

When She Smiles-It paints a picture of a past full of pain
One filled with hopes and dreams which seems never came
But there's this light in her eyes that might surprise and amaze
And When She Smiles it brightens even the darkest of days

When She Smiles it reflects a hint of respect
One she demands from the last bit of regret
She conceals what she feels no scars to detect

Bruises from the chaos that left its mark
Pretty and witty this woman is smart
She can be mean she can be sweet sinister and dark
But there's still remnants of innocence in her misfit heart
And When She Smiles time stands still there's no end or a start

When She Smiles there's miles of tears in her tracks
You can see through the cracks of all her shattered glass
But the past is the past and she ain't ever looking back

When She Smiles you see her confidence as its shining through
A brand new version of a girl she never knew
She lives for her kids and not some dude
And When She Smiles for a while I can't help but smile to……

A love poem from and urban point of view I guess just hoping the girl stays

Will You Stay?

You and I been through so much shit
True grit, down for whatever just for the hell of it
When it comes to us, were both addicted and we'll never quit

No one knows me as well as you
Each other's best friend and everyone knows it too
Love like ours is rare but true
One of these days I might even say I do

You'll never find another me, you've tried with no luck
I've been with other bitches for just a quick fuck
But it could never compare to the way you and me touch

You're my heaven sent my fuckin' curse
But I can always count on you to be there for better or worse
If you die before me they'll need to bring a tandem hearse
Cause I can't live without you and I know it's vice verse

Our hearts may be black but they beat as one
I'll see you in the next life cause we'll never be done
Heaven or Hell we'll always have fun
Unless of course you try to run

Because if you ever try to leave
I'll pour my heart out on your sleeve
This ain't a joke bitch trust and believe

Were trapped in love but that's ok
I want you by my side to ride all the way
Tomorrow, forever, and everyday
So I want to ask and see what you say
Are you down for me baby will you stay?

A dark love tale about breakup and bad relationships and how the girlfriend was basically the devil and how it took a trip to hell to actually understand that.

You Followed Me

My blood stains red, my lips do too
My heart is black, my emotions are blue
My eyes are empty, my soul is dead
Here I lay hallow with a hole in my head
I killed myself on earth and awoke in hell
Pain and misery is all I can smell
The lake of fire, full of screams and agony
Demons are my friends and here's where I'm glad to be
In the distance I see a figure, faint with no sound
As it draws near, I notice it's feet don't touch the ground
Stained with evil and hatred nothing more to be found
Can it really be that <u>you followed me?</u>
Doused in your sorrows forcing me to leave
Heart on my sleeve to the point I could no longer breathe
Dropping to my knees, I plead and I scream
Suicide was the only way to be freed
I accepted it on earth that we were no more
To spend eternity with the devil is my only cure
But I can't believe my eyes, I rub them to be sure
The screams of lost souls pierce my ears
I can't understand why you are here
I see your face, I see it so clear
You was always the devil my biggest fear

This poem was another one written from inside the walls of prison. And although it was a past relationship that didn't work out I still think this was a great poem so I included it in this book it was one I liked because at the time I thought I had this major game plan to come home and do all these great things and had life figured out and just way to confident in my sobriety. But this just goes to show how little we truly know ourselves when we become tested, or we are faced with life's obstacles that we struggle with or fear. Mine proved to be disastrous but I am glad to have learned all the life's lessons that I did and grew to where I am today.

You're All That I Need

Love can be strange, it's usually delayed and comes in waves
And we often look for solace in the things we can't change
Even if it's holding onto the shattered remains
That are broken and hopeless tattered and frayed
And what's worse is it hurts in ways we can't explain
But if you give it to God have patience and pray
Happiness can be found, and great memories made, no matter the case

Looking back in the past we had it rough
Two addicts with bad habits there just was no trust
But we gave up that life and the way we was livin'
And we found ourselves with the help of religion
I put all that bad in the past I promise I'm finished
You're the future I want to last I promise I'm committed
You've been ridin' for me from the start cause your heart has no limit
And just a little bit longer and I'll be home from prison

And although we didn't plan for this to happen
I can't imagine if it hadn't it would have been tragic
I'd be lost without you my life would be madness
So you can't tell me there's no such thing as magic

'Cause if you believe in someone they're worth the fight
And I'm thankful to have been given a second chance this time
But I'm even luckier that you decided to stick by my side
And I'm so excited that we can finally have a life

Together forever let's do this thing right

I don't mean to seem pushy or come off as rude
I'll do my best but I can't stress enough gratitude
'Cause I'll never be able to express or confess to you
My level of appreciation for all that you do
I'm so grateful for your patience and constant support too

So at night time I open my mind to a world I don't want to leave
And I close my eyes just so I can find you in my dreams
'Cause you're everywhere there, like the air that I breath
Your touch is a must it's a constant relief
You won my heart from the start the victory's achieved
I love you baby and "*You're All That I Need*"

www.ingramcontent.com/pod-product-compliance
Lightning Source LLC
LaVergne TN
LVHW041658060526
838201LV00043B/477